H. Sutherland (Henry Sutherland) Edwards

The Lyrical Drama

Essays on Subjects, Composers, and Executants of Modern Opera

H. Sutherland (Henry Sutherland) Edwards

The Lyrical Drama
Essays on Subjects, Composers, and Executants of Modern Opera

ISBN/EAN: 9783744797047

Printed in Europe, USA, Canada, Australia, Japan

Cover: Foto ©Thomas Meinert / pixelio.de

More available books at **www.hansebooks.com**

THE LYRICAL DRAMA.

ESSAYS

ON

SUBJECTS. COMPOSERS, & EXECUTANTS OF MODERN OPERA.

BY

H. SUTHERLAND EDWARDS.

VOL. I.

LONDON:
W. H. ALLEN & CO., 13, WATERLOO PLACE,
PALL MALL, S.W.

1881.

CONTENTS.

———◆———

THE LYRICAL DRAMA.

THE LYRICAL DRAMA.

CHAPTER I.

OPERATIC ORIGINS.

THE opera proceeds from the sacred musical plays of the fifteenth and sixteenth centuries, as the modern drama proceeds from the so-called " mysteries " of the same period. Indeed, the earliest musical dramas of modern Italy, from which the opera of the present day is directly descended, were mysteries differing only from the dramatic mysteries in having been intended for the singing, not for the speaking voice. The opera, or drama in music, is not, compared with the spoken drama, a very ancient form of art. It has somewhere been asserted that the earliest opera on record is the *Song of Solomon*. But this is surely a mistake ; for the work in question, even if it was set

1 *

to music, as to which we are absolutely without information, would not be an opera, but simply a cantata. Solomon and his attractive surroundings have engaged the attention of more than one distinguished composer. But in spite of his wisdom, or perhaps in consequence of it, he never attempted to compose an opera himself.

Persons afflicted with a rage for seeking in the distant past traces and origins of a form of art which was created and forced into existence in comparatively modern times, see the first specimens of opera in the Greek plays; a view which will be worth considering when writers on the subject of Greek music have come to an understanding as to its exact nature. One thing is quite certain, that the Greek plays are remembered solely by what musicians call the "words"; whereas, with the exception of Herr Wagner's highly poetical, highly dramatic works, there are no operas which by their words alone would have the least chance of living. Nor did the musical mysteries or miracle-plays of the fifteenth century — which were partly declaimed, partly sung, and always by the solo voice—bear any great resemblance to the grand operas of the present day, with their airs, duets, concerted pieces, and elaborate and dramatic finales, supported by an orchestra which is always being varied and reinforced through the addition of new instruments, and in which composers aim constantly at the formation of new instrumental combinations. Of course, too, the sacred musical plays of the fifteenth century differed from our modern operas by their subjects. A primitive sort of opera in the *Conversion of St. Paul*, which was performed throughout in music at Rome in 1440, is not the sort of work that would be likely to interest our modern audiences, who entertain a marked preference for operas in which a leading part is assigned to the prima donna, and who have no objection to the prima donna's representing a thoroughly mundane character, such as the fascinating Carmen in the late M. Bizet's opera of that name, or the less fascinating Violetta in Verdi's *Traviata*.

The first opera on a profane or rather on a secular subject—for it is surely a mistake to regard everything not sacred as necessarily profane—was the descent of Orpheus into the infernal regions—drawn thither, as is well known, by his wife Eurydice. The subject of Orpheus, alike lyrical and dramatic, has been a favourite one with composers for the last four centuries, from Poliziano, who produced his *Orfeo* at Rome in 1480, up to Gluck, nearly three centuries later, and from Gluck down to Offenbach, who delights a good many persons in the present day. The *Orfeo* which was brought out just four centuries ago, at Rome, bore no more resemblance in a musical point of view to a modern opera than did the sacred musical plays before spoken of; and up to the year 1600 we meet with no musical work which bears more than a fundamental or general sort of resemblance to the modern opera. But almost immediately after the production of the second *Eurydice*, a great reform appeared. Monteverde, the innovator in question, introduced the modern scale, and changed, or at least gave new developments to, the harmonic system of his predecessors, assigned far greater importance in operas to the accompaniments, and increased greatly both the number and variety of the instruments in the orchestra, which under his arrangement included every kind of instrument known at the time. Monteverde employed a separate combination of instruments to announce the entry and return of each personage in his operas; a dramatic means made use of long afterwards by Hoffman—better known by his fantastic tales than by his musical works—in his opera of *Undine*, and which cannot but suggest a similar device employed with more system and with greater elaboration by Wagner. Monteverde, like so many of his predecessors and followers, felt attracted by the story of Orpheus and Eurydice; and his first work was on the subject of *Orfeo*, which was produced in 1608 at the Court of Mantua, ordered, it may be, by that gallant but dissolute Duke of Mantua whom Signor Mario used to impersonate so admirably in *Rigoletto*. Monteverde's *Orfeo* contained parts for harpsichords, lyres, violas, double-basses, a double harp with two rows of strings, two violins, besides guitars, organs, a flute, clarions, and even trombones. It is interesting to know that apart from the instrumental combinations which announced the entry and return of each character, the bass viola accompanied Orpheus, the violas Eurydice, the trombone Pluto, the organs Apollo, while Charon, —a most unsentimental personage, one would think— sang to the accompaniment of that sentimental instrument the guitar.

I have, of course, no intention of following out the history of opera from Monteverde to Verdi. It will be sufficient for my purpose to remark that Monteverde, the real founder of opera in something like its present form, produced a number of works at Venice, until at last the fame of the Venetian opera spread throughout Italy, so that by the middle of the seventeenth century the new entertainment was established at Venice, Bologna, Rome, Turin, Naples, and Messina.

From Italy opera was introduced into France, where it is popularly supposed to have been naturalised by the Italian scullion and violinist, Lully. It is certain that Lully received from the hands of Louis XIV. a privilege or patent entitling him, and him alone, to perform works in music. But Italian opera had been already introduced into Paris by Cardinal Mazarin or Mazarini, in 1645, and a few years later what was really the first French opera—a work entitled *Akbar, King of Mogul*—was brought out by the Abbé Mailly, who, like Herr Wagner and the Italian composer

Boito in the present day, wrote both the words and the music of his works. The French opera, on the subject of *Ariadni*, was composed by Cambert, a musician who was afterwards driven from France by the intrigues of Lully, and came to England, where he was well received by Charles II., and appointed master of the royal band. Two years afterwards he produced an English version of his *Ariadni*, and although he was not the first musician who brought out operas in England, he was the first who produced operas and directed operatic representations in this country, regularly and continuously.

Opera was introduced into England, in direct imitation of the Italian representations, by Sir William Davenant, who according to some authorities, and, indeed, according to himself—though his evidence on such a point cannot well be accepted—was the son of Shakespeare. The so-called opera of the *Siege of Rhodes*, produced by Sir William Davenant in the dark days—dark, at least, in an artistic sense—of the Commonwealth, seems to have been merely a play with a good number of songs and choruses introduced. These songs were composed by Henry Lawes, of whom I know nothing, except that his name is to be seen on the Albert Memorial in Hyde Park, at the head of a number of obscure musicians to whom England is fancifully supposed to owe such musical reputation as actually belongs to her.

The ruler, then, under whom opera was introduced into England, was Oliver Cromwell. English opera, however, or opera in the English language, has had, from the beginning even to these days, but an intermittent history, and opera in the true sense of the word, that is to say, "opera musicale," or "dramatic work in music," was not firmly established in England until Handel's time, when, aided by a subscription of £50,000, raised for him by some half-hundred aristocratic amateurs, the great German composer introduced Italian opera at the King's Theatre in the Haymarket, where now stands the edifice known as Her Majesty's Theatre. Opera, in fact, whatever its merits or defects, is essentially a royal and aristocratic sort of entertainment. The drama was started by Thespis in a cart, ready, no doubt, to move on at the earliest warning from the police. The opera, on the other hand, was founded by popes, cardinals, and kings. The first operatic libretto, that of Poliziano's *Orfeo*, was the work of Cardinal Riario, nephew of Sixtus IV. Pope Clement XX. was the author of no less than seven libretti. The popes, indeed, used in former days to keep up an excellent theatre, and even in these degenerate days the taste for music has not—or had not until lately—died out at the Vatican. The late Pope Pius IX. frequently invited the Abbé Liszt to stay with him. He took care to have in his apartments an excellent piano; and too polite to ask the eminent virtuoso to perform—seeing that in his case a mere hint would have been a command—used to have the instrument left constantly open, so that the great pianist might play whenever the mood came upon him.

Opera did not come into existence as a growth from below, but as a creation from above. It was artificially produced by potentates and magnates in search of a new artistic enjoyment; but it soon took shape, and need not now be regarded as more unnatural or more unreasonable than any other form of the drama.

The first of the numerous accusations which have at various times been brought against opera in England, did it, oddly enough, incalculable good. When Oliver Cromwell granted Sir William Davenant permission to open a theatre for the performance of operas, we are told by Anthony à Wood that "Though Oliver Cromwell had now prohibited all other theatrical representations, he allowed of this, because, being in an unknown language, it could not corrupt the morals of the people." The "unknown language" was simply music, which, as the language wherein for the first time in England the chief business of a five-act drama was to be conducted, may well have appeared unintelligible. But though opera may not be so plainly intelligible as other forms of the drama, the simple fact of a drama's being performed in music widens its sphere of intelligibility and places it within the comprehension of persons of various countries speaking various tongues. It is the most cosmopolitan entertainment ever invented, and for that reason admirably suited to the wants of the present day. Singers frequently do their best to render it more unintelligible than is necessary; and it is also true that librettists give them powerful aid towards that end by supplying them with words which it is nearly impossible to sing. An opera, however, may be perfectly intelligible as to its general meaning without the words being heard at all. Indeed, those who are over careful as to the precise significance of the words of an opera do not, as a rule, care for the music. They are like those amateurs of painting who think more of the subject of a picture than of its presentment and general execution.

CHAPTER II.

HISTORY OF HER MAJESTY'S THEATRE.

THERE is probably not another lyrical theatre in Europe which has witnessed so many fine operatic performances during so long a period as the "Queen's Theatre" of 1711, which, after being called for a time the "Royal Academy of Music," became the "King's Theatre" on the accession of George I., and retained that name until another alteration of title became necessary when Her Majesty Queen Victoria ascended the throne. In 1710, when Handel arrived in England, the Académie Royale of Paris, at that time under the direction of Rameau, was held in very little esteem, and Italian music was never performed there at all. Indeed, for some sixty or seventy years afterwards, and until the arrival of Gluck in Paris, to be quickly followed by Piccini, the French had the worst opinion of Italian music, which they despised, or perhaps affected to despise. The Queen's Theatre, as directed by Handel, at least during the first years of his management, was, doubtless, not to be compared with the great operatic theatres of Italy. But it soon became the custom to engage for London all the Italian singers of the highest repute; and scarcely an Italian vocalist of real celebrity appeared, from the beginning to the end of the eighteenth century, without, sooner or later, visiting England. Handel, like Shakespere, was not only a great inventor, but an excellent man of business; and though he did not actually introduce Italian opera into England (a few experiments in that line having been made during the five or six years preceding his arrival in London), he it was who first brought out a series of Italian operas, and who organized Italian opera in England on a permanent basis. To his labours as a composer, Handel soon added the functions of a manager; and besides the thirty-five operas from his own pen, he produced, during his connection with our Italian opera, works by Buononcini, Hasse, Porpora, and all the most distinguished composers of the time. At a later period, when the management had passed from Handel to the Earl of Middlesex, the operas of Galuppi, Pergolesi, Jomelli, Gluck, and Piccini, were represented; and all the most eminent vocalists of Europe continued to appear at our London opera-house. After various adventures at Lincoln's Inn Theatre, Covent Garden, the Pavilion, and the King's Theatre, Italian opera found itself once more, towards the end of the century, established at the last of these theatres, which, until Covent Garden was made into an opera-house, did indeed seem to be its natural home. In 1789 the King's Theatre was burned down. It was rebuilt from Novosielski's designs in 1790; and from 1790 until seven or eight years ago, Her Majesty's— formerly the " King's "—Theatre witnessed the production of a long list of works by the most eminent Italian, German, French, and even English composers ; for two operas by Balfe, *Falstaff* and the *Bohemian Girl*, one by Macfarren,' *Robin Hood*, and one by Wallace, *The Amber Witch*, were played at Her Majesty's Theatre during the period either of Mr. Lumley's or of Mr. Mapleson's management. From Handel to Gluck, from Rossini to Verdi, almost every composer of European renown, since the first invention of opera, has appeared at what, since the accession of Queen Victoria, has been known as " Her Majesty's Theatre," either with a new work or with a new arrangement of an old one; and, with the exception of Madame Adelina Patti and Madame Albani, every vocalist who has gained an historic name has, at some time or other, been heard at the opera-house in the Haymarket.

Her Majesty's Theatre, after remaining empty for some years, during which it is reported to have been haunted by the disembodied voices of departed *prime donne* and by apparitions of spectral *ballerine*, has, for the last few seasons, been full of life and activity.

15

CHAPTER III.

THE death of Mr. Frederick Gye, for thirty years the director of the first lyrical establishment in Europe, may be fitly made the occasion of a few words on himself, on the great theatre over which he has ruled so long and so efficiently, and on the influence of his management upon operatic art. Mr. Gye's talents for organization and administration seem to have been inherited from his father, at one time M.P. for Bath, and founder of several highly important commercial enterprises. Mr. Frederick Gye (senior) was the principal partner in the printing firm of Gye and Balne, who held a contract for printing the State lottery tickets. On one occasion a number of tickets which had not been - placed passed into Mr. Gye's hands, either in part payment of his account or otherwise; and the fortunate printer drew a prize of thirty thousand pounds.

Mr. Gye (senior) had now an opportunity of giving full play to his taste for speculation; and his first enterprise, apart from his regular business, was the establishment of the London Genuine Tea Company, the handsome saloon of which was decorated with Chinese views and figure subjects, painted by Clarkson Stanfield and David Roberts. The tea trade was at that time almost entirely in the hands of the East India Company, and Mr. Gye found that it would be quite impossible to compete with these powerful monopolists. His customers were for the most part tea-dealers, wholesale and retail, from the country; and it was in the painted saloon that his clients assembled and that business was transacted. The London Tea Company having made a hit, Mr. Gye (senior) retired from Gye and Balne's, and, besides carrying on the Tea Company, started a Wine Company, and became at the same time lessee and manager of the Vauxhall Gardens.

In the Wine Company and his speculations with regard to Vauxhall Gardens, Mr. Gye (senior) was associated with Mr. Hughes, to whose family Mr. Frederick Gye, manager of the Royal Italian Opera, became allied through marriage. After a time the Tea Company was sold; the Wine Company, owing to an unfortunate speculation in port, of which the principal part of a bad vintage had been bought up, proved a failure, and a series of mishaps was brought to a bad end by a series of very unfortunate seasons at Vauxhall. Mr. Gye retired from Parliament, went to live at Brighton, and remained there apart from speculations, without having the means of engaging in any new one.

Mr. Frederick Gye, after receiving a good public school education, began life with scarcely any advantages except those which his education had given him. He obtained, probably through his father's old connection with the establishment, a contract for lighting Vauxhall; and he held a similar contract throughout a large portion of his life for lighting the Government buildings. Before joining the Royal Italian Opera he was partner with M. Jullien in the Promenade Concerts at Covent Garden; and the Royal Italian Opera had existed but one season, when in 1848 Mr. Gye was called to assist Mr. Delafield, who, on assuming the managership of the Royal Italian Opera, had been required to sell his share in the house of Combe, Delafield and Co., and who was now plunging and floundering on his way to inevitable bankruptcy.

The circumstances under which the Royal Italian Opera was started have been told again and again. Probably the first cause of all in the series of causes and effects which led to the conversion of Covent Garden Theatre into an opera-house was the refusal of Mr. Lumley to engage the famous Persiani for the light parts in Italian opera; these, for several years past, had been assigned to Madame Castellan. It is certain, in any case, that when Madame Persiani had been for some years without an engagement in England, her husband showed himself ready to invest capital in an opposition opera-house. The Royal Italian was started, in a financial sense, by Signor Persiani, and an Italian impresario, named Galetti, with the active support of the great publishing firm of Cramer, Beale and Co. On the 15th of October 1846, an article written by the late Mr. C. L. Gruneisen, well-known as a critic, appeared in the "Morning Chronicle," announcing that the capitalists who had taken Covent Garden Theatre for the formation of an Italian Lyrical Company, had appointed Mr. Beal acting manager and the chief director of the undertaking. During the season of 1848, when the Italian speculators had wisely retired in favour of Mr. Delafield, Mr. Gye accepted the post of acting manager. On the 14th of July Mr. Delafield was made a bankrupt; and Mr. Gye, having previously made an arrangement with the proprietor of the theatre, called principals, band and chorus together, and induced them to perform that night (when the house would otherwise have been closed), on the chance of such receipts as might be obtained. Immediately afterwards it was decided to continue the undertaking on the co-operative principle. At the end of the season Mr. Gye applied for a lease of the theatre; and in September 1849 a lease for seven years was granted to him.

The Royal Italian Opera was still, however, to be managed on the co-operative principle. Mr. Gye was to receive a salary of fifteen hundred pounds a year, and the principal artists were to be paid out of the profits. In 1851, Colonel Brownlow Knox entered into partnership with Mr. Gye, or at least made himself answerable, conjointly with Mr. Gye, for the sum of ten thousand pounds, which was advanced by Messrs. Coutts and Co., for investment in the theatre. In 1853, capital being required, Mr. Thistlethwayte brought into the enterprise twelve thousand pounds, and, going on service in the Crimea, died there during the campaign. In 1856, Covent Garden was destroyed by fire, and the Royal Italian Opera of that season was temporarily established at the Lyceum, where, for the first time, the performances were publicly advertised as taking place under the direction of Mr. Gye.

Going back to the very beginning of the Royal Italian Opera, we find, from the original prospectus, that it was professedly founded in 1847 " for the purpose of rendering a more perfect performance of the lyric drama than has hitherto been attained in this country." The directors proposed to bring out in the course of the first season "some of the established works of Cimarosa, Mozart, and Rossini, and others of the more modern Italian school, including operas by

2 *

Bellini, Donizetti, Mercadante, and Verdi, on a scale
of the utmost perfection in every department, to which
intent the management has assembled a company em-
bracing the greatest and most varied talent in Europe."
Grisi, Persiani, Alboni, Mario, Salvi, Tamburini, and
Ronconi were among the principal artists. In the
orchestra were Sainton as leader, Ella at the head of
the second violins, Lindley as chief of the *Celli*,
Lazarus as first clarionet, and Henry Jarret as first
horn. Mr. (now Sir Michael) Costa, was, it need
scarcely be added, the musical conductor. The direction of the ballet music was entrusted to Alfred Mellon,
and though the new enterprise was intended in a great
measure as a protest against the system pursued at Her
Majesty's Theatre of sacrificing everything to the
ballet, the original ballet company at the Royal Italian
Opera included no less than four *premières danseuses*—
Dumilâtre, Plunkett, Fuoco, and Fanny Ellster. Signor
Maggioni was publicly announced as ready to perform
the high and heaven-born functions of " poet "; and
in one of the first operas produced, that of *I Due
Foscari*, by Verdi, the " poet," in his lyrical translation of the libretto, delivered himself of the following
lines :—

> " Borne by my warm desire,
> To thee would swiftly fly
> My ever constant thought,
> As if the heart was charmed
> By one whom it adores."

The first opera, however, of the opening season (April 6th, 1847) was not *I Due Foscari*, but *Semiramide*, with Grisi, Alboni, and Tamburini in the principal parts. Alboni was entirely unknown at the time; but her delivery of the first few bars of Arcase's introductory recitative at once stamped her as one of the greatest and most richly endowed singers ever heard. The very next season, however, Mdlle. Alboni was replaced by Mdlle. Angri, a lady who would seem to have made her mark further back than was really the case, since Mdme. Angri is now chiefly known as the grandmother of Mdlle. Zaré Thalberg.

The history of the Royal Italian Opera might be written fairly enough from its programmes for the seasons. But allowance would have to be made for the self-congratulatory tone in which it was at one time the fashion to draw up these documents. Thus, when the prospectus for 1851, the year of the first great International Exhibition, was issued, the directors announced that " during the four last seasons the most strenuous exertions of the originators, the directors and the artistes of the Royal Italian Opera, encouraged by generous patronage, have been enlisted in the formation and perfection of this great undertaking, and the present managers have not only the satisfaction of placing at the command of the subscribers a most complete lyrical establishment, but, feeling confident at its undoubted superiority, anticipate the additional gratification during the extraordinary season of 1851, of entertaining a succession of audiences assembled from all portions of the civilised world."

The Repertory of the Royal Italian Opera included at that time no less than thirty-three operas, of which three (*Robert le Diable, Les Huguenots*, and *Le Prophète*) were the work of Meyerbeer. In 1851 (August 9th) Gounod's *Sappho* was produced, this being the first opera by that now celebrated composer which was heard in England. The principal part in *Sappho* was entrusted to Madame Viardot Garcia. But Gounod was to wait for *Faust* to obtain access to this country; *Sappho* was a complete *fiasco*.

During the season of 1852, Rossini's *Count Ory*, Donizetti's *Martiri*, and Spohr's *Faust* (with new recitatives by the composer) were brought out.

For the season of 1853, the first appearance in England of the once famous Mdlle. Joanna Wagner, niece of the illustrious Richard, was announced. But Mdlle. Wagner had signed with two, if not three, London managers; and she ultimately appeared, without making much impression, at Her Majesty's Theatre.

In 1853 Verdi's *Rigoletto*, and Berlioz's *Benvenuto Cellini*, were given for the first time in England. The latter work obtained no success whatever. The Star of Berlioz has lately risen again, but it may be doubted whether *Benvenuto* can be advantageously revived. It failed even at Weimar, under the enthusiastic championship of Liszt.

For the season of 1854, Sophi Cruvelli was engaged, together with the lamented Bosio, whose graceful sympathetic talent now for the first time made itself felt. During this season Madame Grisi gave the first of a whole series of farewell performances, which were only brought to an end by the farewell-taker's obvious inability to sing any more. "It has probably never before fallen to the lot of any candidate for public favour," said the programme-writer of this year, "to sustain for twenty-one successive seasons the highest and most arduous characters of the lyric drama, and most certainly never with such unanimous commendations as have been unceasingly bestowed on Madame Grisi. It is the wish of Madame Grisi," continued the official scribe, " during this her last engagement, to repeat those impersonations in which it has been her good fortune to obtain her greatest success; and it will accordingly be the care of the directors to contribute every possible *éclat* to those performances, relying with the greatest confidence that the subscribers, the patrons of the opera, and the public on this occasion will extend to their long-favoured artiste the cheering influence of their continuance and support."

The puff system was at this time carried to its greatest possible height, and the managers of the

Royal Italian Opera and of Her Majesty's Theatre used annually to try which could 'outbid and out-brag the other.' "It would be difficult," said the directors of the Royal Italian Opera, on putting forth their prospectus for the year 1854, "to express the great satisfaction which they feel (a sentiment which will be doubtless shared by the universal public in general) in being able to announce that they have entered into arrangements with the illustrious Maestro M. Meyerbeer for the performance of his new opera *L'Etoile du Nord*, a work the success of which certainly finds no parallel in the annals of the drama."

1854 was the first year in London of *Il Trovatore*, with Mdlle. Ney, Madame Viardot, Signor Tamberlik, and Signor Graziani as impersonators of the leading characters. This was the year of Signor Graziani's first appearance at the Royal Italian Opera, where he has sung continuously, season after season, for the last twenty-four years.

Early in 1856, as already mentioned, the theatre was destroyed by fire, and for the season of 1856 and 1857, while the house was being rebuilt, the Royal Italian Opera was carried on at the Lyceum. These were the years of the delicious "Opera Concerts" in the Crystal Palace, when the entire band and company of the opera were transferred to Sydenham, to a platform im-provised among the statues, architecture, and shrubs of the tropical end of the nave. The subsequent change of locality to the centre transept robbed these unique entertainments of their peculiar charm.

In 1857 *La Traviata* was produced; not for the first time in England, inasmuch as it had been already played very successfully at Her Majesty's Theatre with Mdlle. Piccolomini in the principal part, but for the first time at the Royal Italian Opera. At Mr. Gye's establishment, where he now proclaimed himself sole director, the principal characters in *La Traviata* were assigned to Mario, Graziani, Bosio, than whose Violetta none more refined has ever been seen on the operatic stage. It had been discovered that the Lyceum was in some respects better fitted for operatic performances than the magnificent building which had been destroyed and was now being rebuilt. Accordingly the prospectus for 1857 pointed out that "some subscribers prefer the small theatre on account of the facility in seeing and hearing the entertainments, as well as for the elegance and exclusiveness of the audiences." Madame Grisi had now returned to give more final performances. The much-regretted Parepa made her first appearance in England, and *Fra Diavolo* was produced, with recitatives and several new pieces added by the composer.

Notwithstanding the preference of so many subscribers for the small theatre, the Royal Italian Opera was transferred in 1858 to the large and magnificent building in which it is still established. In 1858

M. Faure made his first appearance in England, and
Dinorah was produced with Mdlle. Miolan-Carvalho,
Madame Nantier Didiée, Signor Gardoni, and M.
Faure in the chief parts.

In 1860 the Floral Hall was opened, and Gluck's
Orfeo was brought out, with Madame Viardot in the
leading character.

In 1861 Madame Grisi retired for the second but
not the last time. The Grisi parts were assigned to
Madame Penco. During this season Verdi's *Balle in
Maschera* was given for the first time in England with
Penco, Nantier Didiée, Miolan-Carvalho, Graziani, and
Tamberlik in the cast.

The season for 1851 had been rendered for ever
memorable for the first appearance of Madame Adelina
Patti. No one knew anything of Patti until she
stepped on the stage of the Royal Italian Opera in the
character of *Amina*. But long before she had finished
the opening movements of Amina's cavatina, she had
already gained the heart of the public, which, charmed
by her expression, was in the quick movement of the
air to be dazzled by the brilliancy of her execution.

The International Exhibition of 1862 was made the
pretext for an unusually high-toned proclamation to
the subscribers, who were reminded that London would
soon be full of visitors from abroad, and that the opera
" had been, and indeed is still, the delight of foreigners.
It is no longer," added the prospectus, " confined to

the capitals of Italy, France, Germany, or Spain, for in these days Russia, Sweden, Greece, the United States, and South America boast of splendid establishments. There are now also opera-houses in Australia and California, and even the stoled Turks maintain an operatic troupe of some pretensions."

The programme for the season of 1863 was full of congratulations addressed to the subscribers on the happy and auspicious event of the marriage of His Royal Highness the Prince of Wales with Her Royal Highness the Princess Alexandra of Denmark." This was Mdlle. Pauline Lucca's first season in London.

In 1864 it was announced that Lucca, having been brilliantly successful during the previous season, had been re-engaged, and that Patti would "return with fresh laurels gathered during the recess. This young artist," pursued the programme-writer, "has during the past winter visited her native city of Madrid, in which capital she was born on March 19, 1843, and where, as may well be imagined, the display of her wonderful talent was received with the most unbounded enthusiasm by her compatriots." Gounod's *Faust* was produced at the Royal Italian Opera with Lucca, Didiée, Mario, and Graziani, in the principal parts. The character of Margaret was a few weeks afterwards taken alternately by Lucca and by Patti.

L'Africaine was brought out almost immediately after its production in Paris, with the chief parts assigned to Naudin, Faure, Lucca, and Miolan-Carvalho.

During the season of 1867, Gounod's *Romeo and Juliet*, with Mario and Patti as the two lovers, and Verdi's *Don Carlos* (soon to be laid aside), were played for the first time in London.

At the end of the 1867 season, the public was informed that the management of the Royal Italian Opera would probably pass out of Mr. Gye's hands into those of a financial company, which proposed to purchase the interests of the Earl of Dudley and of Mr. Mapleson in Her Majesty's Theatre, with the view of selling the building for conversion into public offices of some kind, and afterwards to purchase Mr. Gye's interest in the Royal Italian Opera, where performances were to be given by a combined company selected from the two establishments. In January 1868 a contract was signed, in which Mr. Gye ceded the Covent Garden property to the financial company for the sum of £270,000. In the opera prospectus for 1868, full particulars of the scheme and of the circumstances under which it had been abandoned were set forth. In 1869 the Royal Italian Opera prospectus was issued conjointly by the directors of the Royal Italian Opera and of Her Majesty's Theatre. The company included Patti, Nilsson, Lucca, Murska, Titiens, Mongini, Naudin,

Tamberlik, Graziani, and Santley. Sir Michael Costa having retired, the directorship was now divided between MM. Arditi and Bevignani. The casts of this season were wonderful. Patti, Nilsson, and Titiens, took the three principal female parts in *Don Giovanni*, and Patti, Lucca, and Titiens, were announced to appear together in the *Marriage of Figaro*. Patti, at the last moment, declined the part of Susanna, and, apart from other reasons, the rivalry between the too numerous *prime donne* would have rendered it impossible for so formidable a combination to endure. It was maintained, however, for two seasons. During the second combination season, 1870, the conductors were MM. Vianesi and Bevignani, Anditi having gone with Mr. Mapleson to Drury Lane, where, pending the rebuilding of Her Majesty's Theatre, Her Majesty's Opera was established.

The last event of real importance in connection with the Royal Italian Opera has been the *début* of Mdlle. Albani, who appearing for the first time in 1872, as Amina (the part in which Madame Patti also sung for the first time before the London public), has gone on constantly progressing in merit and public favour, until she has now for some years been acknowledged throughout Europe as one of the finest singers in the world. If Mr. Gye had done no more than introduce two such singers as Patti and Albani to our public, he would deserve to be remembered with gratitude. But he did more. He maintained the standard of operatic representation at the very high point to which it had been raised by the founders of the establishment, and during a period of management which extended over thirty years, justified the proud language in which the originators of the enterprise had declared, in the spring of 1847, that it was their intention to "render a more perfect performance of lyric drama than had hitherto ¡been maintained in this country."

CHAPTER IV.

THE ROMANTIC AND THE NECROMANTIC.

NECROMANTIC legends have, during the last fifty years, possessed great attractions for operatic composers, several of whom have shown high genius in the harmonious treatment of the diabolical. W. A. Schlegel, in his "History of Dramatic Literature," has given his reasons for preferring supernatural stories to all others as themes for libretti. It seemed to him more natural, or at least less unnatural, that fairies, genii, and other immortals, should address one another habitually in the singing voice than that ordinary men and women should do so. He regarded opera as a fantastic form of art, in which the moving personages should be also fantastic.

Herr Wagner's liking for legends, as operatic groundworks, has quite another origin. Herr Wagner has never troubled himself as to the essential naturalness or unnaturalness of opera, though, as every-one knows, he has denounced with unsparing severity the unnaturalness of operatic works as ordinarily produced. Opera, indeed, like tragedy and comedy, is based on certain conventions, and it is assumed beforehand that in opera the dialogue shall be sung, as it is assumed that in tragedy it shall be spoken in blank verse. It is not, then, because legendary personages belong for the most part to the realms of fancy that legends are especially fitted for operatic setting. Their suitableness for that end proceeds from the fact that they contain dramatic elements which, independently of place or tune, appeal to imaginations. The most famous legends are of universal significance, and are found in all languages, with such variations in details and in external circumstances as the genius of each nation has demanded. This holds true of the most homely popular tales as of the most romantic legends. Thus the principal character in *Le Medecin Malgré lui* is a French woodcutter, while in the Russian version of the same story, of much older date, he is a noble-man of Boris Godounoff's court, who could, without loss of dignity, take a beating from his Czar as Sgana-relle takes his from a landed proprietor in the neigh-bourhood. In the original Sanskrit, the tale, with the same general features, has quite another complexion, but however varied, it is always simple and intelligible.

The legends, however, which seem specially to invite musical treatment are those of a romantic nature, in which the passages are poetical, and in which lyrical emotion springs naturally from the dramatic situations. Upwards of half a century ago, before the production of *Der Freischütz*, it might have been necessary to bring forward arguments upon the subject. But the question has now been practically decided. The leading romantic and necromantic legends of Europe have, since the success of *Der Freischütz*, been nearly all set to music. Herr Wagner has already to dig for his legendary subjects, and as legends can no more be invented than wild flowers can be grown in conservatories, legendary opera must soon come to an end, unless, indeed, the chief legendary subjects already treated should be treated over again, even as such fables as those of Ariadne, Armida, and Dido were set to music again and again in the eighteenth century.

In the history of popular legends, the most ancient of those which have been treated operatically is, doubtless, the *Wandering Jew*. But in the history of music, the oldest is *Der Freischütz*, which has points of similarity with *Faust*, which is obviously connected with *Robert le Diable*, which has something in common with the *Wandering Jew*, which in the family of legends, is closely related to the Flying Dutchman. There are analogies, too, between the story of Tannhäuser bewitched by Venus, and that of Faust sold to the fiend.

I.   3

This, indeed, Tannhaüser himself seems to point out when he affectionately but mistrustfully addresses Venus as a " she devil."

Max, in *Der Freischütz*, shows himself reckless of consequences, provided he can gain an immediate end. His motive is not an ignoble one. He may not even be certain that his mysterious dealings with Caspar will have evil results. But Caspar is a peasant of bad character; and, in addition to his strange appearance and uncanny ways, his power to secure magic bullets should have sufficed to convince Max of his connection with the lower world. Max, then, belongs to the great family of legendary personages who have deliberately sacrificed the future to the present. Max, however, sinned not for the sake of riches, or power, or knowledge, but simply for love, which explains, perhaps, why, without being left unpunished, he was in the end forgiven. Caspar, like more than one diabolical or semi-diabolical personage in necromantic story, suffers from that—

> "Damned equivocation of the fiend
> Who lies like truth,"

by which Macbeth was confounded. The seventh bullet was to kill a human being; and it had never occurred to Caspar that he might himself be struck by it.

With the *Der Freischütz* legend may be compared one of the numerous puppet-show plays on the subject

of *Faust,* in which Mephistopheles binds himself to
his predestined victim faithfully until he shall have
committed his fourth murder. Faust commits two
murders, and no longer feeling bloodthirsty, considers
himself safe. But a snare is laid for him. He finds
Helen of Troy, whom Mephistopheles has brought to
life at his command, in the society of a young man,
and, mad with jealousy, stabs them both. He has
now accomplished his fourth murder, and becomes, as
per agreement, the property of the devil.

The legend of *Robert le Diable* has been so much
altered, and has received such numerous additions at
the hands of Scribe, that only the merest traces of the
original story are to be found in the libretto prepared
ostensibly on that subject for Meyerbeer. Old chroniclers, when they went wrong, which they often did,
seem to have taken pleasure (to borrow a phrase of
Mr. Ruskin's) in being "wrong with precision."
Hollingshead tells us on what day in what year Macbeth's fatal combat with Macduff took place; and who
is to say that Hollingshead and the chroniclers from
whom he derived his materials, were mistaken on the
point? The historian, however, quoted by Scheible in
Das Kloster, who records the doings of *Robert le Diable,*
disposes of his own statements, one by the other, when
he tells us that Robert Duke of Normandy was born
in 763, and that he was the son of Charlemagne.
After that, we are not much astonished to find him

3 *

stating that Robert, who is chiefly known to English-
men as William the Conqueror's father, was, by his
mother's vow, made over to the devil before he was
born, that he was endowed with the power of assuming
the forms of beasts, that he was in the habit of flying
in the air supported by his familiar spirit, and that his
famulus (?) ended by dropping him, when, falling on a
tree, he went to pieces. It is also related of Robert that
he made a pilgrimage to Rome with the view of interesting the Pope in his case and getting the curse under
which he suffered removed; and all these magicians,
at some time or the other, fell in love with a princess.

At Meyerbeer's request, Scribe made Robert and his
familiar spirit the principal personages in an opera
which was originally intended for the Opéra Comique,
and which, like *Der Freischütz*, evidently its model,
contained in its first shape spoken dialogue and no
ballet. When it was afterwards taken to the Académie,
a new, or at least an extended, form was given to it,
the spoken dialogue was put into recitative, and almost
an entire act of ballet was introduced. The added
spectacular scenes may well have spoilt the character
of the work, which is disconnected and extravagant as
now presented. Scribe, however, had endeavoured to
treat his subject as such subjects are treated in mediæval legends of the same description. Bertram, with a
certain likeness to Caspar, bears a greater resemblance to Mephistopheles; and the librettist has no

forgotten that in the popular tale Robert was already before his birth looked upon as a child of the devil. Bertram, in fact, is his father. Robert makes extraordinary journeys, becomes enamoured of a princess, and is saved by Alice, his good angel—much as, in some half-dozen legends, the man who has made himself over to the devil is saved by the favour of the Holy Virgin. Analyse it, and good legendary elements are to be found in Scribe's *Robert le Diable.* But in their artificial combination, they no more make a legend than chemical powders which mixed together effervesce, produce Seltzer-water.

Robert le Diable, however, in the operatic form given to it by Scribe and Meyerbeer, was so successful that the ingenious librettist had no scruple in treating the less promising subject of the *Wandering Jew* as he had treated the Norman legend. Goethe has himself told us how he at one time proposed to deal with the tradition of the *Wandering Jew.* " The legend," as Goethe intended to present it, " ran that in Jerusalem there was a shoemaker named Ahasuerus. The shoemaker, whom I had known in Dresden, supplied me with the main features of this character, and I animated them with the spirit and humour of an artisan of the school of Hans Sachs, ennobling him by a great love for Christ.

" In his open workshop he talked with the passers by, and jested with them after the Socratic fashion; so

that the people took pleasure in lingering at his booth.
Even the Pharisees and Sadducees spoke to him; and
our Saviour himself, and His disciples, often stopped
before his door. The shoemaker, whose thoughts were
altogether worldly, I nevertheless depicted as feeling a
special affection for our Lord, which chiefly showed
itself in a desire to convert this great man, whose mind
he did not comprehend, to his own way of thinking. He
therefore gravely incited Christ to abandon contempla-
tion, to cease wandering through the country with such
idlers, and drawing the people away from their work into
the desert; because an assembled multitude, he said, was
always excitable, and no good could come of such a
life. Our Lord endeavoured by parables to instruct
him in His higher views, but they were all thrown
away on the rough shoemaker. As Christ grew into
greater importance, and became a public character, the
well-meaning workman pronounced his opinion still
more sharply and angrily, declaring that nothing but
disorder and tumult could result from such proceedings,
and that Christ would at length be compelled to place
himself at the head of a party, which certainly was
not His design. And now, when these consequences
had ensued, Christ having been seized and condemned,
Ahasuerus gives full vent to his indignation, as Judas,
who in appearance had betrayed our Lord, enters the
workshop in despair with loud lamentations, telling of
the frustration of his plan. He had been, no less than

the shrewdest of the other disciples, thoroughly per-
suaded that Christ would declare himself Regent and
Chief of the people, and thought by this violence to
compel Him, whose hesitation had hitherto been invin-
cible, to hasten the declaration.   In this persuasion he
had roused the priesthood to an act from which they
had hitherto shrunk.   The disciples, on their side, were
not unarmed; and probably all would have gone well,
had not our Lord given himself up and left them in
the most helpless condition.   Ahasuerus, by no means
propitiated by this narrative, embitters the state of the
wretched ex-apostle, who has no resource left but to
hang himself.   As our Saviour is led past the workshop
of the shoemaker on his road to execution, the well-
known scene of the legend occurs.   The sufferer faints
under the burden of the cross, which Simon of Cyrene
undertakes to carry.   At this moment Ahasuerus steps
forward; and, in the style of those harsh common-sense
people who, seeing a man miserable through his own
fault, feel no compassion, but rather, in their ill-timed
justice, make   the   matter   worse   by   reproaches,
repeats all his former warnings, which he now turns
into vehement accusations, springing, as it were, from
his very love for the sufferer.   Our Saviour answers
not, but at that instant Veronica covers his face with a
napkin, and then, as she removes it and raises it aloft,
Ahasuerus sees depicted the features of our Lord, not
in their present agony, but radiant with celestial life.

Astounded at the sight, he turns away his eyes and hears the words, ' Over the earth shalt thou wander till thou shalt once more see me in this form.' Over-whelmed by the sentence, he is some time before he recovers himself; he then finds that everyone has gone to the place of execution, and that the streets of Jeru-salem are empty. Unrest and yearnings drive him forth, and his wanderings begin."

Scribe, with a view to the special requirements of the Grand Opera, adopted a less naïve mode of presentation, and supplied Halévy with a spectacular and melo-dramatic piece in which all the simplicity of the legend had disappeared, and of which little is now remembered beyond the truly infernal noise made by the newly-invented saxhorns in the final tableau of the Last Judgment.

From the *Wandering Jew*, as treated by Scribe and Halévy, to the *Flying Dutchman*, as treated by Wagner, *il n'y a qu'un pas;* but it is a step which leads, not from the sublime to the ridiculous, but rather from the ridi-culous to the sublime. The Wandering Jew of the ocean—who like his brother on the land, has com-·mitted an unpardonable offence against the Divine Ma-jesty,—*crimen læsæ majestatis divinæ*,—is compelled to sail from sea to sea, until he shall meet a woman who will be faithful to him unto death. The woman he loves proves herself "faithful unto death," by throwing herself into the sea, when, that she may not share his terrible life, he sails away refusing to let her accompany him.   She dies, and the Dutchman, freed from the curse, dies with her.

———————

CHAPTER V.

LYRICAL AND DRAMATIC SUBJECTS: DON JUAN
AND FAUST.

Herr Wagner's theory as to the peculiar fitness of
mythical subjects for operatic treatment, is at least
not contradicted by the exceptional success which two
legendary operas of very different characters—Mozart's
Don Juan and Guonod's *Faust*—have met with in all
parts of the civilised world. Projects have been conceived for showing, and attempts have been actually
made to show, that the two legends have a common
origin; and a German dramatist, the late Christopher
Grabbe, produced a tragedy called *Don Juan and Faust*,
in which the two daring personages, each of whom
provoked relations with the supernatural, figure jointly
as heroes. By a cruel stroke of irony, Herr Grabbe

has furnished a single heroine for his brace of heroes.
He apparently thought that one woman might well
serve for the destruction of both; and his Donna Anna
is made to play the part at once of Donna Anna towards Juan and Margaret towards Faust. In the final
scene, Faust is carried down to the infernal regions by
the Mephistopheles of the piece, who bears no distinctive name, but is called vaguely " the Knight." Having
disposed of Faust, " the Knight" returns, assists
coldly as a spectator at the supper offered by Don
Juan to the statue of the commandant, and when at
last the "Man of Stone" disappears—assuring Don
Juan that he and his assassin will now " meet no more "
—seizes the unrepentant sceptic and bears him off, in
the midst of flames and of Leporello's shrieks, to the
place of torment which has so lately received Faust.
" Now follow Faust," says " the Knight" to his second
victim; adding that, " in different carriages " Faust
and Don Juan had both been " travelling towards the
same goal."

" The Knight's " parting phrase bears, and is doubtless intended to bear, a double meaning. Faust's longing for increased knowledge has rapidly taken the
form of a desire for female beauty, and Don Juan had,
from the beginning, made no secret of the fact that to
him, as at a later period to Richardson's Lovelace,
" girl, not gold," was the chief object of existence.
But say that Faust's offence consisted above all in his

having presumed to question the supernatural powers as Don Juan defied them. Then it was a similar kind of irreligion which led each of these objects of divine vengeance to eternal punishment.

Grabbe, in his little-known work, seems to have intended not only to exhibit synthetically and side by side two legendary personages of the same family, whose points of resemblance had more than once been indicated analytically, but also to combine in the same play two dramatic fables which separately had enjoyed about equal popularity, and of the same kind, one in the north, the other in the south of Europe. Both are of southern origin. But the Faust legend made a powerful impression, and soon became popular with various characteristic and local modifications in Germany, England, Bohemia, and Poland; whereas the Don Juan legend, scarcely appreciated in England and Germany, and never to this day made the subject in either country of any really popular stage-play, was especially cherished and developed in various dramatic forms by the Spaniards, the Italians, and the French.

In literature, the Faust legend has been made the basis of a dramatic masterpiece by an English and by a German poet—by Marlowe and by Goethe; while it has never been treated by a Spanish, an Italian, or a French dramatist. The Don Juan legend, on the other hand, has furnished a theme to Tirso di Molina, who first arranged it for Italian dramatists, and to Molière;

whereas, neither in England nor in Germany did the subject ever inspire one of the great national writers. Shadwell imitated one of the numerous Italian versions of *Don Juan, or the Atheist struck down* (as the popular play was then called) in his *Libertine,* which, besides not being an original work, made no great mark, and was never accepted by the English public, even for a time, with anything like the enthusiasm which the Spanish, Italian, and French dramatic versions of the same story elicited in Spain, Italy, and France.

There is an end to everything, even to a perfect theory; and it is remarkable that, towards the end of the eighteenth century, Mozart, a German, but with a genius scarcely more German than it was Italian, composed an opera on the subject of *Don Juan.* It is equally a matter of notoriety that the libretto of this work was furnished to Mozart by an Italian, da Ponte, and that the said libretto was written in the Italian language. To the last, then, the legend of Don Juan was treated in dramatic shape by an Italian, as, after it had received from a composer of universal sympathies its permanent musical form, the task of interpreting it was entrusted to Italian artists. " Faust " meanwhile continued to be altogether a German or Germanic legend, known to the English as the story of the " Devil and Dr. Faustus," to the Germans as the story of " Faust," to the Poles as the story of " Twardowski " —who, like the mythical Faust, invented printing and

sold himself to the devil. Polish patriots, as in duty
bound, deny the Teutonic origin of Twardowski, and
I have myself seen the pit near Cracow in which
Twardowski and the devil are reported to have held
their unseemly interviews. There are valid reasons
all the same (into which it is unnecessary here to enter)
for regarding "Twardowski" as little better than a
Polish copy of the famous German original.

The end of the Faust legend, if the last artistic word
on the subject has really been said, is a curious one.
After receiving what must undoubtedly be regarded as
its final literary expression from Goethe—who never
intended his *Faust* for stage representation—it was dramatised in the ordinary theatrical sense of the term by
two French playwrights of uncommon ability, MM.
Jules Barbier and Michel Carré. These authors, who
are generally recognised as the most skilful librettists
of our time, turned their very successful French drama
of *Faust and Margaret* into an opera-book, which M.
Gounod, in the spirit less of a philosopher than (as one
of his countrymen has remarked) of a "sensual priest,"
set to music. The result has been that, in these days
of international exchange, the Germanic legend of
Faust has become popularised everywhere through the ·
music of a Frenchman. *Don Juan* and *Faust*, except
in Herr Grabbe's play, are still separate dramas, with
a fundamental idea in common, but with entirely different plots. It can no longer, however, be said that

the southern nations take an exclusive delight in one, the northern nations in the other, of these two modernised miracle-plays. *Faust* is represented at the opera-houses of Milan and Naples, of Madrid and Barcelona, of Paris, and at all the provincial opera-houses of France; while *Don Juan* is played not only as often but much oftener, in Berlin, Vienna, and London, than in the chief towns of France, Italy, and Spain.

⁂ The two most popular legends of mediæval and modern Europe, whatever points of resemblance they may offer, have notable points of difference. Thus, though Faust and Don Juan were equally sure, as Herr Grabbe sets forth, to go to the devil at last, Faust deliberately sacrifices himself beforehand by written compact, whereas Don Juan contracts liabilities, neglects warnings, braves and insults the messenger of justice when his last hour is approaching, and ultimately, without having made any bargain on the subject, incurs the same inevitable penalty as Faust himself. The ultimate fate of Faust is not merely foreshadowed, but is duly marked out for him from the beginning. He is lost before he moves a step. Don Juan, on the other hand, advances gradually from crime to crime, and from scepticism to profanity, until he at last finds himself in a plight which Faust knew from the first must at a given time be his.

Faust, as a whole, is much the more ancient legend

of the two; the story of a man's selling himself to the
devil for immediate and unlimited power, being at
least as old as the sixth century, when the history of
Theophilus of Syracuse, who is alleged to have so disposed of himself, was written by Eutychianus, his
pupil. Some authorities trace the orgin of the story
to Theophilus to certain passages in the Acts of the
Apostles on the subject of magic and the doings of magicians. But a much more probable basis for the legend—
which first became popular through Rutebœuf's miracle-
play of the same name—is to be found in the Gospel
narrative of the Temptation. Theophilus, afterwards
Faust, was ready, for the sake of power, to sell himself to the devil. That is all that the original story of
Theophilus amounts to, except that in the end the
half-reckless, half-prudent man was miraculously saved
through the intervention of the Holy Virgin, whom
personally he had made a point of never offending.

CHAPTER VI.

THE PICTURESQUE SIDE OF THE DON JUAN LEGEND.

THE strange lesson that a man's case is not hopeless whatever he may have done, even to obtaining power on the security of his immortal soul, provided he has not sinned specially against the Holy Virgin, is taught in a very picturesque and pathetic legend of the twelfth century, which suggests at once the story of Theophilus, its direct ancestor; of Faust, its descendant, though perhaps not in a direct line; and of Don Juan, with which it has at least one striking incident in common. It is to be observed, however, that in the devoutly-conceived legend which I am about to relate, the incident in question has not only a different but an opposite signification to that of the incident which, externally considered, so closely resembles it in the diabolical drama of *Don Juan*.

I.   4

" A certain lady," says the author of the tale, " Du bourgeois qui aima une dame " (published in Legrand D'Aussy's " Contes Dévots," extracted and translated from manuscripts of the twelfth century), " wife of a powerful knight, became a widow. Whatever may be said about it, this misfortune is, of all those which a woman may experience, the one she most willingly forgets. For one man that she loses she finds twenty who console her, who call her their lady, their friend, and hasten to wipe away her tears. This one, however, behaved very differently. Young and very agreeable, many gallants solicited her hand in vain. Renouncing marriage, she lived in retirement, wholly occupied with him she had lost.

" Among her admirers was a gentleman of the neighbourhood, rich, full of courage, and handsome in appearance. He visited her and proposed even to marry her; but he was obliged to withdraw, the lady declaring that she wished to remain a widow. After an avowal which left him so little hope, instead of renouncing the object of his love, he was more than ever taken up with it; one might have said that obstacles animated his ardour. Soon there only remained to him the pleasure of seeing his darling when she went to church, or of thinking of her when he did not see her at all. Gradually he lost appetite and sleep, became sad and morose, and took an aversion to life.

" In this condition, he heard of a Jew renowned for

his knowledge of the occult sciences, a great astrologer and necromancer. Numbers of persons congratulated themselves on having been to consult this able man; our lover determined to see him. Does not a sick man believe that each remedy he hears of will cure him? First he thought to conciliate the magician by a present, then he related to him the story of his unhappy love; and he ended by begging him to procure for him the favour of the beautiful widow, promising him a considerable sum if he obtained for him this happiness so much desired. The Jew gave him his word on it; but before all one preliminary condition, hard it is true but nevertheless indispensable, was exacted; that of renouncing God, the Virgin, and all the saints of Paradise. 'Then,' said the circumcised one, 'I will employ to attract your mistress a sure charm: I will render her more ardent than hot coals, and I will see that, of her own accord, she comes and throws herself into your arms.'

"At this proposition the gentleman hesitated for a time. On one side the damnation of his soul; but, on the other, the possession of her whom he loved so much. At last, making up his mind, the gallant offered to deny all the saints and God Himself, without consenting to renounce Our Lady in any manner. In vain the sorcerer represented to him that in a bargain of such importance, one virgin more or less ought not to stop him; the good gentleman persisted in his re-

4 *

fusal, because he knew well that if he kept the Virgin
as his friend, he would one day through her obtain
forgiveness. Through this subterfuge he thought to
catch the devil by reserving to himself a gate of safety;
but his trick was guessed, and he went away without
obtaining anything. On his way home he entered a
church to complain to Her, his fidelity to whom had
just caused him to lose his mistress, and beg her at
least to repair the misfortune she had caused. He approached then an image of Our Lady, said out loud,
' Sweet mother of God, give me her I love, or let it
come to pass that I love her no more.' His prayer
was granted, and the image even bowed its head in
token thereof. Nevertheless, he did not see this sign,
so full was he of his love, but still continued to kneel
and bend his head. But the widow was also in the
church, though he had not noticed her. She, however, saw clearly the action of the Virgin, and she
noticed that each time the gentleman bowed down his
head before her the statue also bent its head. Then she
understood that this Christian was loved by the Holy
Mary and that she did wrong in not loving him herself.

"She followed him as he left the church and asked
him why his countenance was so changed, and in what
places he had been since they had seen one another.
For all answer he told her plainly the whole history of
his love, from her first refusal to his prayer to the

Virgin. ' Mary has rewarded you for your attachment to her,' replied the lady, ' I will be your wife whenever you wish.'

"They were married some days afterwards, and both served Our Lady as long as they lived."

This interesting story contains some elements of the Faust legend, and recals also by the gesture of the statue the miraculous portion of the Don Juan legend ; while the gallant gentleman's idea of cheating the devil by keeping in reserve the good-will of the Virgin, is borrowed from the legend of Theophilus, the progenitor of Faust. There is, I believe, no example in literature of a formal compact with the fiend anterior to the Christian era. But animated statues were known long before the middle ages, and before Christianity itself, which, in a large measure, and wherever the teaching of the Eastern Church prevailed, brought the reign of statues to an end. The most striking feature, then, of the Don Juan legend, though not the legend as a whole, is much older than any portion of the Faust legend.

Indeed, almost the exact counterpart of the insult offered by Mozart's hero to the *gentilissima statua* is to be found in a story told by Pausanias, of Theagenes, crowned fourteen times at the Olympic Games, whose statue after his death was grossly insulted and outraged by a former competitor. The envious rival went so far as to seize the effigy of the conqueror by the beard,

and strike it; on which it fell in vengeance on its
assailant and crushed him to death. Of the sensitive-
ness of Greek statues, even after they had been
adopted by the Romans, a remarkable instance may be
found in Plutarch's Life of Antony; and statues of
purely Roman origin showed themselves equally impressionable and equally human. Immediately before
the battle of Actium, not only at Athens did the statue
of Bacchus (whom, from his moral nature, Antony was
supposed to resemble) fall from its pedestal, but in the
city of Alba "one of the images of stone which was
set up in honour of Antonius did sweat for many days
together; and though some wiped it away, yet it left
not sweating still." The statue of Juno, moreover,
after the taking of Veiæ, entreated by Furius Camillus
to come to Rome and take her place among the other
deities of the Capitol, replied very distinctly, both by
gesture and by word of mouth, that she would do so.

The good-natured, semi-religious, semi-rationalistic
Plutarch did not quite believe in these tales of talking
statues, which, as a faithful chronicler, he gives for
what they may be worth as they reached him and as
they were repeated by others. He relates in his "Life
of Coriolanus" that, when the ladies of Rome built
their temple to Fortune, the image of the goddess
"did speak as they offered her up in the temple and
did set her in her place." "And they affirm," he continues, "that she spake these words: 'Ladies, ye have

devoutly offered me up.' Moreover, that she spake twice together, making us to believe things that never were and are not to be credited." He then proceeds, in quite modern fashion, to explain, at least to some extent, the miracles he has recorded, but which he cannot swallow, in the form traditionally belonging to them. "For to see images," he says, "that seemed to sweat or weep, or to put forth any humour red, or bloody, it is not a thing unpossible; for wood and stone do commonly receive certain moistures whereof are engendered humours which do yield of themselves or do take of the air many sorts and kinds of spots and colours; by which signs and tokens it is not amiss, methinks, that the gods sometimes do warn men of things to come. And it is possible also that these images and statues do sometimes put forth sounds like unto sighs and mourning when in the midst or bosom of the same there is made some violent separation or breaking asunder of things blown or devised therein; but that a body which hath neither life nor soul should have any direct or exquisite sounds formed in it by express voice, that is altogether unpossible."

Plutarch himself, then, as interpreted by North, believed it to be "unpossible" that a statue should speak. Probably, also, like Goldoni at a later period, he held it to be contrary to nature that a statue should bow its head, walk, and go out to supper; for Goldoni, in his common-sense and slightly common-place version of *Don Juan,* has carefully suppressed the miraculous part of the legend.

One of Lucian's dialogues contains a good story of the statue of a Corinthian General which every night used to get off its pedestal and walk through the streets, and which further resembled our friend the statue of the Commander by its habit of singing— though not, we may suppose, to an accompaniment of trombones. The Corinthian General interfered with no one who did not interfere with him. But it was advisable not to get in his way; and if he had been mockingly asked to supper—above all, if he had been pulled by the beard, like the statue of Theagenes, and like the statue of the Commander in the original Don Juan legend, his vengeance would doubtless have been terrible. The amiable unprovoked statue of the Corinthian General presents no very apparent moral resemblance to the statue of the Commander. Tournefort, however, in his "Voyages," tells a story not of a statue but of an image or cikon in relief, representing St. George on horseback, which used periodically to play the part of Avenger not only towards those who had directly offended it, but towards all wrong-doers, more especially perjurers and breakers of promises, real or implied. This miraculous image of St. George decorated the walls of a Greek convent in the island of Scyros, and when service was celebrated in the convent church would leave its habitual resting-place, and, "although very heavy," says Tournefort, "would hover in the air above the congregation ; when if anyone was present who had made a vow to the church and had not yet accomplished it, it found him out in the crowd, placed itself upon his shoulders, and gave him repeated blows on the back and head until he paid what he had promised."

St. George of Scyros, in making war on the demon of infidelity, did not confine his attention to church-goers nor the sphere of his activity to the convent church. He travelled about the island, not flying, as the superstitious might believe, but carried on the shoulders of a blind monk. The monk could not, of course, know where he was going; but St. George mysteriously directed him, so that whenever a perjurer or a debtor was to be found, there in due time arrived the blind monk with St. George upon his shoulders. The unhappy man could not escape; but when once it had reached him, the image fell upon him and beat him until he paid.

CHAPTER VII.

THE DON JUAN LEGEND—*continued.*

On ne badine pas avec l'amour. Statues of Venus, as
of the Holy Virgin, must not be trifled with. Next to
pulling by the beard the effigy of a dead hero, or of
asking it to supper, no more dangerous offence is recorded in the history of the dealings of men with statues, than that of treating with levity the sculptured
figure of the Pagan Virgin or of the Christianised
Venus.

When Pope St. Gregory attained the Pontificate,
there were still a great many pagans at Rome. The
Pontiff, fearing they might be tempted to adore the
numerous statues of saints, male and female, distributed
throughout the town, caused all the marble figures to
be collected in one of the public squares. One day

when some young pagans were amusing themselves by
wrestling in this open space, one of them, recently married, having taken off his wedding ring, which he was
afraid of injuring, put it for safety on the finger of one
of the statues, saying at the same time, in jest,
"Woman, I take you for my wife." Now this was
the statue of the Virgin. Our Lady, who had no idea
of being joked with, took the young man at his word,
and bent her finger, so that when he wished to take
back his ring, it was impossible to get it off.

Nor was that all. At night, thinking his wife was
by his side, he was very much astonished to find himself laid hold of by a powerful hand, which pressed his
body in a painful manner. At his shrieks his terrified
wife rose, and went for a light. While she was away,
Our Lady appeared to the young man, and declared
herself to be the wife whom he had taken that morning before witnesses. She called upon him to be faithful to her and to have nothing to do with his first wife.
The pagan thought there must be witchcraft in all
this. As soon as it was daylight he called a priest to
exorcise the supposed demon. The priest arrived with
stole and holy water, told the young couple to fear
nothing, and felt sure that as long as he with holy
water remained near them the devil would not venture to appear. But Our Lady returned, saying
plainly that she cared neither for priest nor holy
water, and that she would not, under any circum-

stances, tolerate infidelity towards her. The husband and wife went in great distress, and told the whole story to Pope Gregory, who, lest the Church should be suspected of being powerless in the matter, forbade them absolutely to speak of it. Meanwhile, he counselled the young man to keep his wife at a distance, a piece of advice which was far from pleasing to him. Sometime afterwards a hermit recommended him to consecrate one day of the week to the praise of the Virgin, who, appeased by this compensation, ordered him in a fresh apparition to erect a statue exactly like the figure he at that moment beheld. At first the Pope objected; but on the prayers of the bridegroom, threatened in subsequent visions with exemplary punishment if he remained obstinate, permission was granted, and the statue was solemnly dedicated to St. Mary of the Rotunda. Thereupon everyone was astonished to see a ring on her finger. Recognising it as his, the husband begged her to give it up to him. She consented, and he lived happily with his wife for ever afterwards.

"This miracle proves," adds the old monk from whom Legrand d'Aussy borrows the tale for his "Contes Dévots," "how good Our Lady is; but it also shows that it will not do to trifle with her, still less to be wanting to her in respect."

Prosper Mérimée has shown in an admirable tale, clearly derived as regards main idea and even prin-

cipal incidents from the above, that Venus also must
not be trifled with, that she is not to be made use
of for a moment and then forgotten, but that she
will " attach herself to her prey," and perhaps destroy
it in her embrace. There is no appeasing the pagan
deity; and in " La Vénus d'Ille " the imprudent wrestler
who has placed his ring on the finger of the Goddess of
Love, is crushed to death in her brazen arms. So at
least it would seem. But the incidents of the mysterious drama take place long after the age of miracles ;
and all that the narrator of the story knows for certain
about the matter is that cries were heard in the night,
and heavy thumps at regular intervals on the staircase,
going first upstairs and after a time down again. The
next morning the statue of Venus is where it was before,
with the same malicious smile on its lips, which the
chronicler of the story had noticed when, arriving in the
character of wedding guest, he saw it for the first time.

A miracle drama or dramatic sketch, of the thirteenth century, *Li Jus de Saint Nicholai*, by Jean
Bode, introduces a statue of St. Nicholas, which is
slighted, through a denial of its miraculous power as
to the protection of property, but is neither personally
insulted, like the statue of Theagenes and that of the
commandant, nor trifled with like those of Venus and
of the Holy Virgin. In *The Game of St. Nicholas*, a
prisoner called " le Prud'homme," after a defeat of
the Crusaders, is brought before the King of Africa,

and by him threatened with a cruel death. Le˙ Prud'-
homme throws himself down before the figure of St.
Nicholas, Bishop of Myra, who, it must be observed,
wears his mitre, and, discovered in this position by the
" Seneschal," is brought by that functionary before the
king.

" *The Seneschal.*—King, to show you a wonder, we
have kept him alive. Now let me tell you what he has
been doing. I found him praying on his knees, with
clasped hands, before his horned Mahomet King. Say,
villain, do you believe in him?

" *Le Prud'homme.*—Yes, sire, by the holy cross, I
do. It is right that everyone should pray to him.

" *King.*—Tell me why, ugly villain.

" *Le Prud'homme.*—Sire, it is Saint Nicholas who
succours the afflicted; his miracles are unmistakable.
He repairs all losses to the person invoking him, re-
places in the right path those who have strayed; recals
evil-doers to God, restores sight to the blind, resusci-
tates the drowned. If a thing is entrusted to his keeping, it will neither be lost nor will it deteriorate, however much it may be exposed. It would be all the
same were this palace full of gold, if Saint Nicholas
stood over it. Such is the grace that God has given
him.

" *King.*—Villain, I will soon test that. Before I go
away from here your Nicholas shall be put to his trial,
I will entrust my treasure to him; and if I lose as

much as would go into my eye, you shall be burned, or broken on the wheel."

Thereupon the public crier announces that the king's treasure is no longer under lock and key nor in any way guarded, except by a "horned Mahomet, who is quite dead, and cannot move a peg." Cliquet, Rasvir, and Pincedé, professional cheats and thieves, hasten to profit by the announcement, and before long have carried off the treasure of the King of Africa. The statue meanwhile neither moves nor speaks.

" What is it, by Mahomet? Who wakes me up? " cries the King, when the Seneschal hurries to his bedside to tell him the result of the experiment.

" King," answers the Seneschal, " you are a pauper and reduced to beggary. But you can blame no one since you chose to confide your treasures to the care of a man of wood. He is now lying on the ground."

The Prud'homme is about to be hanged, and the executioner has already placed the rope round his neck, when he begs for one day's respite, which the merciful King of Africa grants. The Prud'homme prays to St. Nicholas. St. Nicholas appears to the robbers in their sleep and terrifies them; the treasure is replaced, and is found next morning as if intact, with St. Nicholas on the top of it; the Prud'homme is saved, and the King of Africa, called upon to give his heart " to God and to the Baron St. Nicholas," exclaims:—

" St. Nicholas, I am your man, and I renounce

Apollo, Mahomet, and that rascal Tervagan. Let us all be baptized as soon as possible, for I can truly say that I serve God."

The statue or image of St. Nicholas, avenged by St. Nicholas in person, is presented, as already mentioned, in a miracle-play of the thirteenth century. The statue of the Virgin, which declined to allow itself to be trifled with, and the statue of the Virgin which bowed its head to the gentleman who, though he gave up his soul, yet refused to renounce the Holy Mary, belong to legends of the century before. The Don Juan legend, in its various forms, is later than all these. Not, however, that it has its origin in mere fable. According to the Spaniards, the story of Don Juan, which after a time assumed a mythical and miraculous physiognomy, and which might well have owed its existence in the first instance to earlier traditions of the same kind, is based on facts decorated with a certain number of falsehoods; not falsehoods such as every fact destined to become the nucleus of a legend gets surrounded by, but falsehoods deliberately invented for the purpose of concealing a crime.

"It came to pass one day," says the "Chronicle of Andalusia," "that a hare-brained young fellow, Don Juan Tenorio, a scion of one of the Twenty-Four of Seville, killed with a sword-thrust the Venerable Commander Uloa, whose daughter he had carried off. The illustrious warrior was buried in the Convent of St.

Francis, where his family had a chapel. A statue was erected to him. The Franciscan brothers seeing that the murderer found in the privileges of his birth a pro-tection against justice, resolved to remedy the power-lessness of the laws, and accordingly enticed him at night into their convent and put him to death. Then they spread the report that Don Juan had dared to brave and insult the Commander in his tomb, and that his statue, becoming suddenly animated, had precipi-tated the impious man into the flames of hell."

Quasi-historical facts, however, are often invented to explain legends which, properly regarded, need no such explanation. Probably, the genius of the southern nations, and equally of the Slavonians, who are southern by temperament, inspires them with visions of living men and real incidents where northern nations would see little more than dreams and shadows. No Ger-man would have the hardihood to declare that Faust lived in this or that place; it would be scarcely less absurd to point out the *casta dimora* in which dwelt the perfectly modern Margherita to whom, according to M. Gounod, Faust addressed his love-songs. The Poles, however, have a local habitation as well as a name for their Polonized Faust; and Twardowski's favourite spots near Cracow are marked in the guide books.

As for Don Juan, there is so little doubt among Spaniards as to his having really lived, that several cities dispute the honour of having given him birth. Only two centuries ago, when the numerous Don Juan dramas were still new, the remains of the statue of the Commander were to be seen at Seville; and not more than twenty or thirty years since, a young Spaniard, who claimed to be Don Juan's lineal (and legitimate) descendant, visited the national library at Paris, with the object of collecting information on the subject of his family.

CHAPTER VIII.

THE ORIGINAL DON JUAN: DON JUAN IN SPAIN.

Don Juan was not an honourable man himself; but he lived so long ago, that it would be considered a great honour in the present day to be descended from him. In fact, a young Spanish nobleman calling himself Don Juan Tenorio presented himself, only twenty-five years ago, at the National Library of Paris for the purpose of consulting documents which he hoped might throw some new light on the history of the notorious and not altogether fabulous personage whom he claimed as his ancestor. " Handsome and singularly prepossessing in appearance," says M. Castil Blaze, who relates this incident in his notes on Molière's " Festin de Pierre," " tall, graceful, equally distinguished in gesture and speech, the attendants had already addressed him *sotto voce* as Don Juan when he declared himself to

5 *

be a descendant of the hero of Tirso de Molina, of
Molière, and of Mozart. This was Don Juan Tenorio
who came in person to seek in our literary archives
historical notes on his family.

The Don Juan of 1850 was not preceded by any
statue, and he had perhaps left Catalino, Arlequin,
Phillippin, Carrille, Sganarelle, Camacho, or Leporello
in his cab at the door of some Parisian Donna Anna.

The National Library of Paris, in fact, contains four
copies of a work on the nobility of Andalusia ("No-
bleza de Andaluzia en Sevilla," por Fenando Dray,
1588) by Goncalo Argote de Molina. In this ancient
chronicle a brief mention is made of Alfonso Jufre
Tenorio, Admiral of Castello, "one of the great men
of his time," a longer account of this personage and of
the Tenorio family generally being promised in the
third portion of the history, which, however, was never
completed.

The author did not even finish the second part, as
appears from the following note written in the catalogue
of the National Library, by Clément, the under-
librarian, in 1700, " *Secundam et tertiam hujus operis
partem parabat sed non perfecit; decessit non benè sanâ
mente, parvâ re domesticâ.*" The Don Juan Tenorio of
1850 had sought in vain for the missing volumes in the
libraries of Spain, and hoped to be more fortunate at
Paris, where, however, he was again to be disappointed.

It is unnecessary to inquire whether the Argote de Molina, who deals with the origin and early history of the Tenorio family in his nobiliary records, was a relative of the Tirso de Molina to whom the first drama on the subject of Don Juan is due, for Tirso de Molina is known to have been a pseudonym adopted by Gabriel Tellez, a friar of the Order of Mercy, and commander of the monastery of Sovin. Whether the legendary Don Juan was or was not an historical as well as a legendary personage is a question which at least may be entertained. It is certain, in any case, that the family of Tenorio, to which Don Juan is said to have belonged, was a family of importance in Spain towards the end of the sixteenth century. It seems difficult to identify the man, and it may fairly be assumed that Argote de Molina, writing in 1588, had never heard of that Don Juan Tenorio who was punished by the statue of the Commander he had slain, or he would at least have taken some notice of such a remarkable occurrence. Tirso de Molina's or Gabriel Tellez's drama was publicly performed in 1622, and a religious play or mystery on the same subject, if not from the same hand, had been previously acted in the Spanish convents.

Keeping, however, to ascertained dates, let us assume that the story of Don Juan was first placed before the Spanish public in the drama composed by the head of the monastery of Sovin. Even if some Don Juan of real life did indeed demean himself more or less in the style of that Don Juan afterwards presented on the stage, he must have done so between the date of the publication of Argote de Molina's nobiliary chronicle in 1588 and that of the first performance of Tirso de Molina's play in 1622.

The fact that Don Juan was accepted in Spain as the dramatic reproduction of a gentleman lately deceased, and that the statue which supped with him on the stage was a faithful copy of a statue which, in a somewhat dilapidated condition, could actually be seen, may not prove that the story of Don Juan had a true historical basis. It is interesting, however, to know that at a time when Don Juan was looked upon as a genuine historical personage, and scarcely more than fifty, the remains of his terrible foe, the statue of the Commander, were actually in existence more than fifty years after the man of pleasure and the man of stone were first exhibited in conflict on the stage. " A gentleman who has just returned from Spain," says a writer in " Le Mercuro Galant" (1677), "has explained the story to me. It is there, he asserts, that the adventure really happened, and the remains of the statue of the Commandant may, he assures me, yet be seen. But that does not prove that the statue moved its head and came to take its seat at the table with the Don Juan of the comedy, as the Spaniards were the first who put this subject on the stage. Tirso de Molina, who thus treated it, gave it this title, *El Combi-*

dado de Piedra, which has been very badly rendered by " Le Festin de Pierre." The Spanish words signify nothing more than " Le Convié de Pierre," that is to say, the " Marble Statue invited to Supper." The title of Molière's comedy, which itself was borrowed from that of a whole series of French comedies on the subject of Don Juan, derived from the Spanish through the Italian, has puzzled many of Molière's commentators, while it has fairly baffled his translators. Mr. Cowden Clarke, in his " Molière Characters," renders " Le Festin de Pierre " by " The Feast with Don Pedro," which is a mistake, but a mistake made not without authority. Mr. Van Laun, in his excellent version of Molière, prefers " The Feast with the Statue," which is ingenious, but is also wrong. The " Guest of Stone " is the proper title or second title of the work; but this, of course, would not be a translation of the " Festin de Pierre."

The name of the original Spanish drama by Tirso de Molina is *El Burlador de Sevilla y Combidado de Piedra,* " The Scoffer of Seville and the Guest of Stone." The action of Tirso de Molina's drama takes place at Naples, where, to borrow Mr. Van Laun's account of the plot, a certain Duchess Isabella, of whom Don Juan, under the feigned name of Duke Ottavio, has taken advantage, complains loudly to the King, who orders the guilty one to be seized. The seducer escapes, and is shipwrecked on the coast of

Tarragona in Spain, where he meets a young fisher-
man's daughter, Tisbra, whom he seduces under promise of marriage, and who, when undeceived, throws
herself into the sea. We next meet him at Sevilla,
where, under the name and the disguise of his friend
the Marquis de la Mota, he treats Donna Anna, the
daughter of the Commander de Uloa as he had treated
Isabella. He then kills the Commander and anew
takes flight into the country, where he meets Aminta,
who also falls a victim to his usual method of promising marriage. Don Juan secretly returns to Sevilla,
and sees in the church the mausoleum of the Commander de Uloa bearing the inscription, " Here the
most loyal of gentlemen awaits until God shall avenge
him on a traitor." Don Juan and his servant Catalino
insult him, and invite him to supper. The statue
makes its appearance, and requests Don Juan to come
to feast with him the next evening at 10 o'clock in the
chapel. He goes, and the seventeenth scene of the
third day's tornado shows us the funeral feast in which
Don Juan and the statue sup on scorpions and vipers,
drink gall and vinegar, and in which finally the libertine repents and asks for a priest to be confessed and
to receive absolution. The last scene of the play represents the Alcazar at Seville, where the King repairs
the crimes of Don Juan by giving all his victims away
in marriage, and commands the tomb and statue of the
Commander to be brought to Madrid to remain there

as a warning for all time. The Spanish Don Juan is not a heartless and deliberate seducer, a thorough unbeliever; but an easy-going fellow, swayed by his passions, who does not repent because he thinks he has sufficient time for that, and who, at the final catastrophe, proves himself a good Roman Catholic. Moreover, he meets the statue, not because he disbelieves in miracles, but because he has given his word to come, and " the dead man might otherwise have the right to call him infamous."

The impression which the Spanish play leaves on the mind is eminently a religious one, and must have been strongly felt at the time it was written—a result enhanced by the scene in the chapel with the moonlight shining through the stained glass windows, and the chorus singing, " Let those who flee from the punishments of God know that there is no term nor debt which must not be paid. No mortal living should say, ' I have time before me '; the time for repentance is so short."

CHAPTER IX.

DON JUAN IN ITALY.

THE story of Don Juan was treated very seriously in
Spain, both by the unknown author of the mystery or
" auto sacramental " called *L'Ateista fulminata,* and
by Gabriel Tellez, otherwise Tirso de Molina, who produced the first regular drama on the subject. Translated into Italian, Tirso de Molina's *Burlador de
Sevilla* lost, in the hands of Onofrio Giliberti, much of
its sombre and all its religious character. It was
shorn, too, of several scenes, notably of the opening
one at Naples, in which Don Juan, after seducing the
Duchess Isabella, abandons her, and embarks for Spain.
The number of Don Juan's victims is thus diminished
by one. Isabella, however, was not to be forgotten by
subsequent dramatists. She reappears in Molière's *Don*

Juan, ou le Festin de Pierre, under the name of Elvira,
and, as Elvira, has been immortalised in Mozart's opera.
Tisbea, the Fisher-maiden, who, like the " Schönes
Fischermädchen " of Heine's poem, is made to see in
the agitated bosom of the ocean the emblem of a heart
disturbed by love, becomes Rosalba in the Italian play.
In Molière's comedy, as in Lorenzo da Ponte's libretto,
the Tisbea of the Spanish, the Rosalba of the Italian
drama, has entirely disappeared ; though some traces
of the marine beauty may, perhaps, be found in the
beauty of the fields whom Molière introduces, under
the name of Mathurine, as rival to Charlotte—the
Aminta of the Spanish drama, the Zerlina of the
Italian opera—in the lively scene where Don Juan,
placed between the two, plays the part afterwards to be
enacted by our own Captain Macheath, pestered by Polly
on the one hand, by Lucy on the other.   The nominal
list of Don Juan's mistresses, or rather, the women
whom he has deliberately betrayed, was an idea of
Giliberti's, and belongs neither to Tirso de Molina's
drama, nor to Molière's comedy, which, with much that
is original, contains scenes imitated partly from the
Spanish, partly from the Italian.   Don Juan's father,
whom Molière preserved, so that, besides representing
his principal personage as a seducer, a murderer, a
scoffer, a spendthrift, and a cheat, he might also exhibit
him as an unnatural son, was probably thought too
gloomy a figure by the Italians ; and we all know that

Lorenzo da Ponte did not think him worthy of a place in his admirable libretto which gives us the most compact and most dramatic presentation of the Don Juan incidents, as Molière's comedy gives us the most complete and most philosophic study of Don Juan's character.

It was not Giliberti's *Convitato di Pietra*, produced at Naples in 1652, but a very droll imitation of that work by Torelli and his company of burlesque actors, which, presented at Paris in 1657, first made known and at once popularised the subject of Don Juan in France. The Italians were followed by a troop of Spaniards, who, two years later, performed the original Spanish play *El Burlador de Sevilla*, from which a host of Italian and French pieces, serious, serio-comic, and grotesque, were to be derived. In nineteen years no less than five French versions of *El Burlador de Sevilla*, or rather of *Il Convitato di Pietra*, were brought out, all of which, except the last (the versified edition of Molière's *Festin de Pierre*, by Thomas Corneille), seem to have been known to Shadwell when, in 1676, he composed, on the great dramatic theme of the period, his *Don John, or the Libertine destroyed*.

In the *Convitato di Pietra*, as played by Torelli's company, the piece opens with a conversation between Harlequin, Don Juan's servant, and the King, on the subject of Don Juan's vicious life, which is followed by a ludicrous soliloquy for Harlequin—the Catalino of

Tirso de Molina's drama, the Sganarelle of Molière's comedy, and the Leporello of Mozart's opera. Harlequin, wrapped in a black cloak, carries a long Spanish sword, at the end of which shines a lantern. He has not yet finished his burlesque reflections when he is startled by the sudden arrival of his master, at whose approach he lets the lantern fall to the ground, and thereupon follows its example. Don Juan, wondering what this noise can mean, draws his sword. Harlequin stretches himself out on his back and raises his weapon straight in the air, so that whatever way his adversary turns in fencing, he still finds its point opposed to him. At last Harlequin drops his sword and cries out that he is killed. Don Juan, who recognises him by his voice, asks him whether he is really dead. " Don Juan!" replies Harlequin, " I am still alive; if not, I am defunct."

Don Ottavio now enters accompanied by Pantaloon, his faithful attendant. While Don Ottavio and Don Juan exchange compliments, Harlequin walks up to Pantaloon, and at every opportunity makes him a low bow. Pantaloon, confused by so much politeness, moves away. Harlequin follows him, recommences his salutations, but at the same time practises the sword exercise under cover of his cloak, and suddenly, when Pantaloon least expects it, deals him a blow in the stomach which brings him to the ground. Harlequin falls over him. They rise together. Then Harlequin steals Pantaloon's handkerchief and wipes his nose with

it. Pantaloon sees him, and a scuffle takes place, in
which Harlequin is, of course, victorious.

Don Ottavio is on the point of marrying Donna
Anna, and has promised to visit her that evening. Don
Juan will not hear of this. He persuades Don Ottavio
to change cloaks with him so that each may go out
freely on his own adventures. Harlequin does the
same with Pantaloon; and no sooner have Don Ottavio
and his faithful valet left the stage, than Don Juan
declares that he has only taken Don Ottavio's cloak in
order that he may more easily deceive Donna Anna.
Harlequin protests, on which Don Juan boxes his ears
and orders him to do all he is bid without comment.
Harlequin having been stationed as sentinel at the
door, Don Juan enters the house of the Commander,
Donna Anna's father. At his daughter's cries, the old
man appears in his shirt, and thus lightly attired, pursues Don Juan, sword in hand. Arrived in front of
the stage, Don Juan and the Commander fight despe-
rately until the latter falls, mortally wounded. Harlequin takes fright, stumbles over the body of the
dead man, picks himself up, and at last runs away.

Donna Anna now complains to the King, who, in
reply to her appeal, begins by offering ten thousand
pounds and the pardon of four brigands for the name
of the Commander's murderer. The proclamation
suggests to Harlequin some ideas which make Don
Juan doubt his fidelity. He threatens to kill the

rascal if he dares to open his mouth on the subject. Harlequin swears eternal secrecy. " But if you were put to the question?" says Don Juan. " Still not a word," answers the Harlequin. "We'll soon see," continues Don Juan, who, assuming the tone of the executioner, pretends to be about to torture him, on which Harlequin at once divulges all he knows. Don Juan repeats his menaces, and wishes, for safety, to change clothes with his valet, when the latter runs off, followed by his master. In the second scene, Pantaloon, convinced that Harlequin knows the assassin, endeavours to make him confess. " If the King offered you the reward himself, and produced you the pardon of four of your best friends, who should you say it was?" he asks. " I should say it was you," answers Harlequin ; and he then proposes that Pantaloon shall allow himself to be accused of the murder and take half the reward. The first act ends with the arrival of the police, who offer Harlequin a purse of money if he will tell them where his master can be found. Harlequin pockets the money, gives false information, and takes to his heels.

In the second act, Don Juan, in a characteristic expedition, has had the misfortune to be shipwrecked. But he reaches the shore, and is picked up by Rosalba (the "Schönes Fischermädchen" before mentioned), in whose arms he takes care to faint. Harlequin floats in on a barrel, calling out for wine " after so much water," and, seeing how Don Juan is engaged, says that "if ever he falls into the sea again, he hopes he may be saved on such a bark as that." Don Juan, meanwhile, to reassure the gentle Rosalba, swears, and calls Harlequin to witness, that if he fails to marry her, he hopes he may be killed, "not by a live man, but by a man of stone."

An hiatus (*valdé deflendus* by poor Rosalba) now occurs. On her reappearance, "Unhappy girl," says Harlequin, "to believe in my master's promises. If he goes to hell, which sooner or later must happen to him, he will try to seduce Proserpine. If he had remained much longer in the sea, he would have made love to the whales." "You promised to marry me," says Rosalba, "and I expect you to keep your word." "Impossible," replies Don Juan. "Speak to this honest gentleman on the subject, he has my entire confidence." Don Juan disappears and Harlequin produces the record of his master's conquests—a long roll of parchment, which he throws before him as he unfolds it, so that the further end reaches the middle of the pit. "Look, gentlemen," he cries to the audience; "just see whether, by chance, the name of your wife, your sister, or your sweetheart is not among them." He then adds to the list the name of Rosalba, who, in despair, throws herself into the sea

Now comes the scene with the peasant girl—the Zerlina of Mozart's opera. "Receive my congratulations, Signor Cornelio," says Don Juan to the bride-groom. "That is not my name," replies the young man. "No, but it soon will be," replies Don Juan, as he goes off with the bride. The scene changes; the statue of the Commander appears; and the invitation to the supper is given and accepted as in the opera.

The third and last act commences with a scene in which Harlequin lectures his master through the medium of fables and burlesque apologues. "I remember," he says, "reading in 'Homer's Treatise on the Art of preventing Frogs from catching Cold,' the story of a sucking-pig at Athens, which possessed such charming qualities that, instead of being put on the spit, it was educated with the greatest care, treated most tenderly, and fed on biscuits and macaroni." Harlequin goes on to relate how the little pig broke into a flower garden, destroyed the rarest plants, the most beautiful flowers, and yet was forgiven; how it upset everything in the kitchen, and was still pardoned; until at last it made its way into the dining-room one day, when company was expected, and smashed dishes, glasses, and decanters full of the most exquisite wines. Then, losing all patience, the master had it killed, and converted it into pork, ham, bacon, sausages, pigs-fry, and black-pudding. "The master of the pig represents 'Jupiter,'" says Harlequin, "the pig, O my venerated master, is you; while the gardener, the cook,

I.   6

the crystal goblets, and the porcelain vases, are the victims of your misdeeds." Don Juan pretends to be touched by Harlequin's preaching—which, by the way, may have suggested the more serious hypocrisy manifested by the Don Juan of Molière's comedy. Harlequin falls on his knees to thank " Jupiter " for his master's conversion (the censorship would not have tolerated the introduction of the Christian deity), when Don Juan recalls him to a sense of reality by his customary medium of a kick.

Supper is now served, and Harlequin is seen in all his glory as a practical jester. First of all he announces that the kitchen chimney is on fire. Don Juan and the servants leave the room in haste, and while they are attending to the imaginary conflagration, Harlequin devours the best things on the table. Driven away with blows, he procures a fishing-rod, and, from the other end of the stage, hooks a roast fowl. Beaten once more, he pacifies his master by telling him of a charming widow, whose acquaintance he pretends to have made. That he may be able to keep an appoint. ment with her easily, he persuades Don Juan to let him sit by his side and take a hurried meal. " Now, rascals, look sharp ! " he calls out to the other servants, as he takes his seat. In reply to Don Juan's interminable and of course interested questions about the widow, he only answers in monosyllables, that he may not be too much interrupted in his eating. Among other feats of voracity, he swallows twelve raw eggs, calling out after each for a glass of wine. In mixing the salad he empties a can of vinegar into the bowl, and adds the contents of four salt-cellars, a quantity of mustard, all the oil in the lamp, and finally the lamp itself. Then becoming meditative, he reflects on the inconstancy of fortune. "Imagine," he says, "that this piece of meat at the end of my fork is a man, borne aloft on the wheel of prosperity. One turn, and down he falls into the abyss!" Uttering these words, he swallows the delicate morsel.

He goes out to see the widow, but returns, declaring that she is not at home. "You lie," says Don Juan. "If I do," replies Harlequin, "may this piece of venison choke me." "And her maid?" asks the master. "She, too, had gone out," answers the valet. "If I deceive you, may this glass of wine poison me." A knock at the door is now heard. The statue of the Commander has arrived.

6 *

›

CHAPTER X.

THE ITALIAN DON JUAN IN FRANCE.

THE statue of the Commander is received in the Italian plays, as in Mozart's opera, by Don Juan's knavish attendant. First a footman goes to the door, but returns, half paralysed by fear, and, tumbling against Harlequin, almost upsets him. To show that he is equal to the situation, Harlequin takes up a roast fowl in one hand, a candlestick in the other, and hurries to discover what has frightened the lackey. But the sight of the statue fills him with such terror that he hastens back, and in doing so overturns half-a-dozen servants. As he can scarcely speak, Harlequin now indicates by nods that the stone figure which he had asked to supper, and which had bowed its head in reply, has really arrived. He then gets under the table. Don Juan takes up a light and goes forward to welcome his visitor, saying, as he leads him into his banqueting-room :—"If, my honoured guest, I could have believed that you would really come to supper, I would have ransacked Seville for bread, Arcadia for meat, Sicily for fish, Phœnicia for birds, Naples for fruit, Spain for gold, England for silver, Babylon for carpets, Bologna for silk, Flanders for peas, and Arabia for perfumes, that I might have offered you a table sufficiently splendid to be worthy of your greatness. But accept what I present to you with a warm heart and a free hand—Eat, O guest."

Harlequin is now forced to come out of his hiding-place, and ordered to sing and drink to one of his master's favourites. In obedience to Don Juan's signs he names Donna Anna, the Commander's daughter, stands up, fills his glass, and looks towards the statue, which acknowledges the compliment by bowing its head. Harlequin, in his alarm, turns over head and heels backwards, holding the glass of wine in his hand, and—if he does the trick properly—finds himself once more on his feet, without having spilt a drop. Tomaso Antonio Vicentini is said to have executed this feat of strength and skill with marvellous dexterity.

In all the Don Juans presented on the stage up to the time of Mozart's opera (except, of course, the rationalistic version prepared by Goldoni), Don Juan pays a return visit to the statue, which thus appears in three different scenes. The audience could not, it must have been thought, behold too often the portentous Man of Stone. The last act—or at least one scene in the last act—of all the pre-Mozartian Don Juans takes place in the Commander's tomb; and in Torelli's "trage-comedy," the profligate hero, accompanied by the lively Harlequin, presents himself in due time at the last abode of the courteous old nobleman who, like Lucrezia Borgia at a later period, knows how to reply to one act of civility by another, and who, in lieu of an "orgia," offers his late host a supper with the worms.

All around him being dark, Harlequin observes, as he enters the tomb: "The washerwoman of the house must be dead; everything here is so black." From a plate of roast meat offered to him Don Juan takes up a serpent, exclaiming: "I would eat it if it were the devil"—a sign that Don Juan, as one might have inferred from his character, has an excellent digestion. Mysterious and mournful chants are now heard. The statue rises, the thunder growls, the earth opens, the flames of hell are seen, and the Man of Stone descends with the scoffer into the abyss. Harlequin, in despair, utters his famous exclamation: "My wages, my wages! Must I send a bailiff to the devil for my wages?" The King, already seen in the first act, now reappears. Harlequin, who had not approached His Majesty since his reception at the opening of the drama, falls at his feet, and says: "You know, O prince, that my master has gone to the devil, where all you great lords will go one of these days. Reflect, then, on what has taken place." A final tableau exhibits Don Juan in the midst of torments appealing to the demons, who in reply to his entreaty to be informed when his sufferings will come to an end, "if ever," reply in chorus, "Never!" The concluding scene between Don Juan and his tormentors was alone in verse. The rest of the piece was entirely in prose, and in prose of which a portion every evening was improvised.

In Torelli's *Convitato di Pietra* Harlequin's practical jokes and verbal sallies were, nearly all, of Italian invention, including in particular his cry of despair on Don Juan's descent into the infernal regions, "My wages, my wages!" an exclamation which, though it was tolerated and even applauded in Spanish and Italian, was forbidden by the Paris censorship when Molière put it into the mouth of the French Sganarelle. Neither Sir Aston Cockain, in his *Tragedy of Ovid*, nor Shadwell, in his *Don Juan, or the Libertine destroyed*, seems to have thought the servant's ingenious exclamation worth reproducing. In the former work, however, a reminiscence may be seen of Harlequin's (and Catalino's) facetious remarks about the blackness of everything at the funeral repast given to Don Juan in the Commander's mausoleum.

"This table," says Catalino, pointing to the tomb-stone of black marble on which the repast is spread, "is so black that it must have come from Guinea; or else there can be no one here to clean it." In the *Tragedy of Ovid*, by Sir Aston Cockain, who, after the manner of adapters, made needless changes in the scenes he appropriated, and who substituted the skele-ton of an executed criminal for the traditional statue of the Commander, the banquet offered to his Don Juan (otherwise "Captain Hannibal") by the "Spectre" is served on "a table covered with a black linen cloth, all the napkins of the same colour, the meat and dishes, bottles, wine, and all things also"; and "Cacala," the Catalino, Harlequin, or Sganarelle of the piece, thereupon observes:

> "I do not like the colour of this linen;
> The meat and wine and everything is black."

To which the absurd Spectre replies:

> "'Tis the sole colour used in Pluto's Court."

The Italian authors omitted the final scene of Tirso de Molina's drama, in which, immediately after the catastrophe, all the remaining personages, with the ex-ception of Donna Anna, appear on the stage. Donna Isabella of Naples, Tisbea the fisher-maiden, Aminta the peasant girl, come forward, each accompanied by her lover, to demand justice of the King, who orders

that Don Juan be put to death by the victims of his
perfidy. The venerable Don Tenorio, in spite of the
crimes committed by his more than prodigal son (*Le
Fils Criminel* is one of many titles, or sub-titles, under
which the piece used to be played in France), begs that
he may be permitted to die in his place, when, suddenly, Catalino rushes in with the news of Don Juan's
terrible end.

" Since the cause of so many disasters is dead,"
says the King, "each one will do well to marry his
betrothed," a course to which no one makes the least
objection. The Marquis de la Mota (who corresponds
to Don Ottavio in the opera, as Isabella corresponds to
Elvira, and Aminta to Zerlina) goes off to look for
Donna Anna, the only one of the ladies whose honour
remains intact; Catalino declares his intention of becoming a monk; and the King orders the tomb of
Gonzalo de Ulloa to be removed from Seville to
Madrid, that the memory of the illustrious statue may
be cherished by "a larger population." It is to be
observed that in Tirso de Molina's drama the statue of
the Commander does not adorn a public square, as in
Mozart's opera, but decorates his own tomb in the Church
of the Franciscans. It is in this church that the infernal banquet of scorpions and vipers is given to Don
Juan. It may also be observed that in the fourteenth
century, when, according to the " Chronicle of Seville,"
the incidents of the Don Juan story really occurred,

Madrid, instead of being the capital of Spain, was only a small village.

The one scene of importance in the Italian version of *Don Juan*, which the authors had neither borrowed nor imitated from Tirso de Molina, was that in which Harlequin exhibits to the unhappy Rosalba, the heroine of the sea-shore (Tisbea in the Spanish play) the list of Don Juan's mistresses. A similar catalogue of conquests is spoken of, but not shown, in Ben Jonson's "Cynthia's Revels," a work of much earlier date than the earliest of the published "Don Juans," and earlier by at least half a century than Giliberti's *Convitato di Pietra*, in which the long roll of deluded and deserted women was for the first time substantially introduced. Ben Jonson's Amorphus boasts that he has been successful in love with "three hundred forty and five, most of noble, if not princely descent, all of whose names," he adds, "I have in catalogue." The *catalogo delle belle*, turned to such excellent account by Giliberti, and afterwards by Lorenzo da Ponte, by Mozart, and by more than one eminent Leporello, was not adopted by Molière, who in his *Don Juan*, contents himself with making Sganarelle say, with regard to the number of his master's victims : "*Dame, demoiselle, bourgeoise, paysanne, il ne trouve rien de trop chaud, ni de trop froid pour lui; et si je te disais le nom de toutes celles qu'il a espousées en divers lieux ce serait un chapitre à durer jusqu'au soir.*"

Molière's rejection of the formal and seemingly interminable chronicle of victims shown by Don Juan's servant to the latest on the list, has been accounted for, more or less satisfactorily, by his supposed unwillingness to treat a theme which had been already exhausted, and which Torelli's actors had dealt with, night after night, in the most extravagant spirit of burlesque. M. Henri Van Laun, Molière's English translator, adopts this view, which, as far as I know, was first put forward by M. Castil-Blaze in his "Molière Musicien." Molière, according to M. Castil-Blaze's suggestion, might possibly have reproduced the catalogue, could he have taken it direct from the hands of Giliberti. But the Harlequin of Torelli's company had added to it so many pleasantries of his own; he had so enlivened it with verbal and practical jokes of every description, and often of the wildest kind, that Sganarelle, exhibiting the familiar list in the tone of comedy, would have appeared tame. This explanation may seem sufficient. But it must also be remembered that Molière, though a free borrower, was a copious inventor, that some five or six versions of the *Guest of Stone*, in Italian, Spanish, and French, had been played at Paris when he undertook to produce a *Don Juan* of his own; and that, while retaining the chief personages, the central incidents, and, of course, the catastrophe of the original Spanish play, he departed in many points from the story as told by his predecessors,

and introduced new characters and new scenes entirely of his own creation. Molière may have wished
to show that he was not obliged to follow in the
steps of previous adaptors. At the same time, he
must, as a practical dramatist, have felt it desirable to
avoid presenting to the public a whole series of scenes
with which they were already familiar.

It has been seen that Don Juan, on quitting Spain
for the first time, visited Italy. From Italy he travelled to France, entering by way of Lyons, where, in
1658, he appeared for the first time in a French dress
(imitated from the Italian), at a representation offered
to the Court of Louis XIV. But an Italian Don Juan
(Torelli's burlesque version of Giliberti's piece) had
already been seen at Paris in 1657; and in 1659 the
original Spanish Don Juan (*El Burlador de Sevilla*)
arrived. That same year a second French Don Juan
was introduced, so that before Molière's Don Juan
was brought out, the Paris public had been enabled
to make the acquaintance of Don Juans of a great
many different kinds and speaking three different
tongues.

CHAPTER XI.

MOLIÈRE'S DON JUAN.

IT would be a mistake to suppose either that Molière's *Don Juan* was derived directly from Tirso de Molina's *Burlador de Sevilla*, or that Mozart's *Don Giovanni* was founded on Molière's *Don Juan*. These three presentations of the Don Juan legend stand out from among some twenty or thirty others; that of Molina as the first regular drama on the subject; that of Molière as the Don Juan of literature, and that of Mozart as the Don Juan of music. In all three we find Don Juan, his indispensable servant, and the still more indispensable statue of the Commander. But the tragic figure of Donna Anna introduced in Tirso de Molina's play, and which acquired such high dramatic significance as treated by Lorenzo da Ponte and Mozart, was omitted by Molière, who equally neglected, or, for reasons of his own, did not choose to reproduce, the scene of the Commander's death, with which the opera so effectively commences, and which has its place also in *El Burlador de Sevilla.*

No such scene as that in which Leporello displays the list of Don Juan's mistresses, occurs either in Tirso de Molina's drama or in Molière's comedy; the idea of the *catalogo delle belle* having been borrowed (as already mentioned) from the *Convitato di Pietra* of Giliberti, with whom it seems to have originated. It would be dangerous, however, to express a decided opinion on this point. Mérimée's Don Juan de Marana (in *Les Âmes du Purgatoire*, the incidents of which are from Spanish sources) keeps such a catalogue for his own private gratification. We have seen, too, that in a play of Ben Jonson's, produced more than half a century before Giliberti's piece, a personage of the Don Juan type boasts of having been successful in love with three hundred, fifty, and five women (we are still very far from Leporello's "*mille e tre*") whose names he has "in catalogue"; and it is quite possible that Ben Jonson and Giliberti may both have been indebted for their catalogue notion to some old Italian or Spanish author. A similar catalogue to that of the Italian Don Juan, in whose family (to the exclusion of the Spanish and French branches) it has been preserved, is introduced in La Fontaine's *Joconde,* of which the subject matter is known to have been de-

rived from Ariosto. In his " Dissertations critiques
sur l'Aventure de Joconde racontée par Arioste, par
La Fontaine et par Bouillon," Boileau, after showing
how far the main incidents of his story " La Fontaine "
was indebted to the " Orlando Furioso," adds, not,
however, that the things which he has himself added
may not be placed on the same parallel with all that is
most ingenious in the original story : " Such is the invention of the blank register which our two adventurers
carry with them for inscribing the names of those by
whom their advances may not be repelled. This pleasantry seems quite as amusing as the rest of the tale."

La Fontaine's *Joconde*, however, was published in
1665, the year in which Molière's *Don Juan* was produced on the stage, and eight years after the first performance in Paris of the *Convitato di Pietra*, as given by
Torelli's company, in which Arlecchino's catalogue
formed so important a feature. It is evident, then, that
although La Fontaine was not indebted for Joconde's
register to Ariosto, he yet did not invent this detail
himself. " Il nous faut," says Joconde to his Esquire
Astolfe :—

> " Il nous faut, dans notre équipage,
>   Continua le prince, avoir un livre blanc,
>   Pour mettre les noms de celles
>   Qui ne seront pas rebelles,
>   Chacune selon son rang.
>   Je consens de perdre la vie
>   Si devant que sortir des confins d'Italie
>   Tout notre livre ne s'emplit."

In fact, after a time,

> "Il n'est dans la plupart des lieux
> Femme d'échevin ni de maire,
> De podestat, de gouverneur,
> Qui ne tienne à fort grand honneur,
> D'avoir en leur registre place."

In literature the author of an idea is he who first makes effective use of it; and Giliberti must be regarded as the originator of Don Juan's catalogue until the title can be established of some earlier claimant as yet unknown. Ben Jonson's mention of such a catalogue as being kept by his hero Amorphus is at least suspicious. He may really have imagined it and not, free borrower though he was, have been indebted for it to some Italian source—from which in that case Giliberti might also have drawn. However this may be, the catalogue which struck the fancy of La Fontaine, and which furnished Mozart with the subject of an admirable piece of music, was first presented on the stage and employed as a dramatic means by Giliberti.

As for Molière, the task which he had set himself was the production of a new *Festin de Pierre* when two *Festins de Pierre* were already in existence; of composing a *Don Juan* of his own, and insuring its acceptance by a public already acquainted — besides the French versions — with one Spanish and two Italian *Don Juans*. Accordingly he turned to the five contemporary works on the same subject, less to see what he could take from them than to discover what he must absolutely avoid. The dramatic scene for Don Juan, Donna Anna, and her father, the Commander, had been presented often enough, and could no longer be counted upon to produce its original effect. The catalogue of beauties, so fertile a source of "gags," had also been done to death. Finally, the worst of all, the Statue had been much over-worked, and the two banquets, out of which the Torelli company had extracted so much fun, rendered absolutely impossible. Molière, however, did what no other dramatist would have been able to accomplish—he gave to the public a *Don Juan*, not, indeed, with the character of Don Juan omitted, but with all the most striking scenes in the familiar story left out, and with the part of the Statue reduced within the very narrowest limits. In Molière's *Don Juan, ou Le Festin de Pierre*, the important characters are Don Juan and his servant Sganarelle; and Don Juan engages our attention at least as much by what he says as by what he does. He becomes the full and finished portrait of a powerful, unprincipled nobleman, who, apart from his courage and chivalrous bearing, has no good point in his character; and who, besides being exhibited as a seducer and scoffer, is shown to us as a fraudulent but most plausible debtor, which in real life, circumstances urging him thereto, he naturally would have been; and

I.   7

who ultimately, in his last stage of corruption, appears as a hypocrite.

Beaumarchais might, or rather must have had Molière's *Don Juan* in mind when he traced the character of Count Almaviva. But Figaro is in a much more direct manner a development of Sganarelle, and many of Figaro's reflections on a noble's privileges and their abuse are little more than amplifications of reflections uttered in the same spirit, though in a somewhat different tone, by Sganarelle.

"I tell you, between ourselves," says Sganarelle, "that Don Juan, my master, is one of the greatest scoundrels upon earth, a madman, a dog, a demon, a Turk, a heretic, who believes in neither heaven, hell, nor devil, who passes his life like a regular brute beast, one of Epicurus's swine, a true Sardanapalus who shuts his ears against all Christian remonstrances that can be made to him, and considers all we believe as so much nonsense. You tell me that he has married your mistress; believe me, he would have done more to satisfy his passion, and would, besides herself, have married you, her dog and her cat into the bargain. It costs him nothing to contract a marriage, he uses no other snare to entrap the fair sex; and he marries whomsoever he can get hold of." "If a great lord," says Sganarelle, soon afterwards in the style of Figaro serious, "is a wicked man, it is a terrible thing."

After the caricature of Don Juan drawn by the

valet, to whom he is no hero, we have Don Juan painted by himself.

" A nice thing," he says, "to pique oneself upon the false honour of being faithful, to bury oneself for ever in one passion, and to be dead from our very youth to all the beauties that may strike us ! No, no, constancy is only for fools; every handsome woman has a right to charm us, and the advantage of first being met with ought not to rob others of the just pretentions which they all have upon our hearts. As for me, beauty delights me wherever I meet with it, and I easily give myself up to that sweet violence with which it hurries us along. It does not matter if I am engaged ; the love I feel for one fair does not induce me to do injustice to others ; I have eyes to see the merit of all, and pay to each the homage and tribute which nature demands from us. However it be, I cannot refuse my heart to any lovely creature I behold, and as soon as a hand-some face asks it of me, if I had ten thousand hearts, I would give them all."

So a later Don Juan wished that women had but one pair of lips among them that he might kiss them all. "Budding inclinations," continues the Don Juan of Mo-lière, "have a charm which is indescribable (' en amour,' George Sand has written, ' il n'y a que des commence-ments '), and all the pleasure of love is in variety."

Beamarchais's Figaro, asking the typical French nobleman of the days before the Revolution, what he

7 *

has done to deserve his privileges, replies to his own question, " *Vous vous êtes donné la peine de nâitre.*" So the virtuous Don Louis, Don Juan's father, speaking of his son's noble birth, says to him :—

"Tell me, pray, what right you have to be proud of it? and what have you done in this world that gives you a claim to be considered a nobleman ? Do you think it sufficient to bear the title and arms of one, and that it is any glory to be descended from noble blood if one lives in infamy ?"

Equally in the style of Figaro, when Figaro talks politics, are Sganarelle's remarks on the imaginary Don Juan, whom he supposes to be something quite different from the Don Juan he has the honour of serving :—

" Had I a master of that kind, I would tell him plainly to his face : ' Dare you thus jest with heaven ? and do you not tremble to laugh as you do at things most sacred ? . . . Do you think that because you are a man of rank, because you wear a fair and well-curled wig, have some feathers in your hat, a gold-lace coat and flame-coloured ribbons (I do not speak to you but to the other), do you think, I say, that you are a cleverer man for all this, that you may be allowed to do everything, and that no one should dare to tell you the truth ? ' "

There is something very subtle in Don Juan's adoption of hypocrisy as a cloak to screen himself from censure when his misdeeds have raised such an outcry that he finds it inconvenient any longer to meet it by mere bravado. He does not, however, deceive himself; and he calls upon Sganarelle to witness that policy, not principle, induces him to assume the devout air which so little becomes him, and which, at the earliest opportunity, he hastens to throw off.

Besides the admirable monologues and dialogues which serve to exhibit the character of Don Juan as it had never been exhibited before, Molière's play contains several entirely new scenes. The finest of these is the famous one in which Don Juan appears as a sceptic, not without compassion. The " Poor Man," whom Don Juan has met in the wood, declares that his occupation consists in praying to heaven for all kind people who give him something :—

" You are pretty well off then? " asks Don Juan.

" Alas, Sir," says the poor man, " I am as poor as poor can be."

Don Juan.—" You are joking. A man who prays to heaven every day must be very well off."

Poor Man.—" I assure you, Sir, that frequently I have not a piece of bread to eat."

Don Juan.—" That is strange. Your assiduity is ill-rewarded. Ha! ha! I am going to give you directly a piece of gold, provided you swear a round oath."

Poor Man.—" Oh, Sir! would you wish me to commit such a sin? "

Don Juan.—" Will you gain a piece of gold? yes, or no? Here is one for you if you swear. There; now swear."

Poor Man.—" Sir!——"

Don Juan.—" Unless you swear, you shall not get it."

Sganarelle.—" Well, well! Swear ever so little; there is no harm in it."

Don Juan.—" Take it; here it is. Take it, I tell you; but swear."

Poor Man.—" No, Sir, I would rather die of hunger."

Don Juan.—" There, there. I give you this piece of gold for the sake of humanity."*

Somewhat similarly, in Octave Feuillet's "M. de Camors," the hero of that tale, who possesses some of the characteristics of Don Juan, tempts a rag-picker with a twenty-franc piece, which he throws into a heap of mud, promising to give it to him if he will pull it out with his teeth. The rag-picker, having humiliated himself in the manner described, M. Feuillet's Don Juan relieves himself by formally permitting the " poor man," " for the sake of humanity," to knock him down.

The last of Molière's new scenes for stage effect,

---

* In Mr. Van Laun's translation, of which, with the exception of the last five words, I have made use, " *pour l'amour de l'humanité,*" " because you are a human being."

and also, perhaps, the most diverting, is that in which Don Juan makes love alternately to the two peasant girls, Charlotte and Maturine, as a century later Captain Macheath, in our *Beggar's Opera*, was to make love to Polly and Lucy. The scene, however, between Don Juan and his creditor belongs to a higher style of comedy. After M. Dimanche has been kept waiting a considerable time (though without the knowledge of Don Juan, who holds that it is very bad policy to hide from creditors, and that an able man "should possess the secret of sending them away satisfied without giving them a farthing"), the bourgeois, who has in this case no pretension to be considered a gentilhomme, is introduced, forced to take a seat, and overwhelmed with compliments. The moment allusion is made to the account, Don Juan congratulates M. Dimanche on his healthy appearance; then, when M. Dimanche returns to the threatened subject, inquires after his wife, and hearing, to his delight, that she is quite well, wards off another advance by asking news of M. Dimanche's little daughter, Claudine. "What a pretty little girl she is," he continues, "I love her with all my heart."

M. Dimanche.—"You do her too much honour, sir. I——"

Don Juan.—"And does little Colin make as much noise as ever with his drum?"

M. Dimanche.—"Always the same, sir. I——"

Don Juan.—" And your little Brusquet? Does he still bark as loudly, and as lustily bite the legs of the people who visit you ? "

M. Dimanche.—" More than ever, sir, and we cannot break him of it."

Don Juan.—" Do not be surprised if I ask after your whole family."

And so on, until, at last, without once allowing him to speak of the bill, Don Juan asks M. Dimanche to supper, an invitation which the confused tradesman, perhaps with a presentiment that he might meet strange guests at Don Juan's table, hastens to decline. He then disappears, accompanied by his courteous debtor to the door.

It may be doubted whether Molière would not willingly have dispensed with the statue had it been possible not to employ its services. There is nothing either of the romantic or of the grotesque in Molière's *Don Juan*, which for the first time exhibits the hero of the story as a perfectly consistent profligate, believing, as Sganarelle says of him, neither in heaven, hell, nor devil. Accordingly, in Molière's play, the statue of the Commander appears more as the symbol of divine punishment than as a personage playing an interesting and striking part in a supernatural drama. Molière's final scene consists only of three short phrases for the statue, and three equally short for Don Juan, who dies as he had lived, and as a

dramatist of Molière's genus could not fail to represent him, unrepentant and defiant. He sinks with
the statue, Sganarelle calls out that his wages are not
paid, and all is over.

Molière's comedy gave great offence. It was considered intolerable that Don Juan should be made to
utter speeches precisely in the spirit of his actions.
His crimes had long been accepted as by no means
unfitted for stage representation. It was the enunciation of the principles by which alone his misdeeds were
to be explained that raised general indignation. Molière's Don Juan analyses himself, sets forth his own
private views and motives, turns himself inside out, in
a word, after the manner of Shakespeare's leading personages; and as, besides being a seducer (which would
have been forgiven to him), he is also a cynic, sceptic
and scoffer, his views are not edifying.

The doubts hinted by Don Juan as to the efficacy
of prayer in the scene with the "Poor Man," were
found particularly shocking, and had to be omitted.
Sganarelle's exclamation on the subject of his unpaid
wages was excised by the Censor on the ground that
to think of wages in the presence of an awful manifes-
tation of divine wrath, was to give proof of a callous-
ness too revolting for exhibition on the stage. It had
been endured on the part of the Italian Arlecchino,
but the licensing authorities probably held that what
would do but little harm in a foreign tongue might,

spoken in the vernacular, prove a source of grave scandal. Similarly, I believe, our own Lord Chamberlain will sometimes pass in French what he would feel bound to condemn if it came before him in plain English.

In modern times, French dramatic censors have occupied themselves chiefly with the political bearing of pieces submitted to them, and have shown themselves lenient, not to say lax, on religious points. In the seventeenth century, however, the Church, which in previous centuries had allowed the drama, in the shape of mysteries, to slip from beneath its absolute direction, could still enforce some measure of respect from its escaped child. It could, at least, prevent the ridicule of sacred things on the stage, or even the introduction into dramatic dialogue of religious expressions. " God" —as in English plays of the present day—had to be replaced by " heaven "; and for " heaven " the plural " heavens" was often substituted.

In Italy the censorship was stricter even than in France. Accordingly, Arlecchino, in *Il Convitato di Pietra*, as played by Torelli's company, not daring to speak on the stage of " God," " heaven," or even " heavens," and wishing to caution his master against the wrath of heaven, called upon him to beware of the wrath of " Jupiter." Similarly, the devil was called " Pluto," and hell " Hades." In the Italy of the seventeenth century, it was hazardous even to mention the Christian Virtues on the stage; and in prefaces to Italian plays of this period—the period of *Don Juan*—readers are requested to observe that such words as "Grace" and "Charity" are used not in a religious sense but merely as "poetical expressions."

To introduce, however, in connection with Don Juan, the anger of Jupiter, the offended majesty of Olympus, and the terrors of Hades, was to commit anachronisms of some significance. It may be doubted whether in the pagan world the gods would have been much scandalised by Don Juan's goings on—which were, at least, not worse than those of Jupiter himself. A Roman gentleman might have behaved as badly as Don Juan, both towards women and towards men (the point as regards statues may be reserved), without exciting much indignation on the part of contemporary society, and certainly without calling down upon himself the vengeance of heaven. Mark Antony, for instance, behaved quite as badly as Don Juan. No one, however, objected to him much on that score. His biographer, Plutarch, seems to have had no suspicion that his life may have been deserving of serious blame.

Apart from the outcry raised against Molière's *Don Juan* on quasi-religious grounds, the general public, accustomed, in connection with dramatic works of importance, to the charm of verse, seems to have been unable to reconcile itself to the fact that Molière's *Festin de Pierre*, with the exception of a few speeches from the more dignified characters, was written in prose. Accordingly, " Mademoiselle de Molière," soon after her husband's death, employed Thomas Corneile, son of the illustrious Pierre, to versify it, and Thomas Corneille's rhymed edition of Molière's masterpiece replaced, at the Théâtre Français, the original prose version, until some thirty years ago, when the great literary and philosophical Don Juan was restored to its due position in its original shape.

CHAPTER XII.

DON JUAN IN ENGLAND.

IT was not until after four *Festins de Pierres* in French, *Il Convitato di Pietra* in two Italian versions, and *El Burlador de Sevilla* in Spanish, had been ˙played at Paris, that any drama on the theme, which possessed so much fascination for the three great literary nations of southern Europe, was offered to the public in England. Shadwell, however, in 1676, eleven years after the production of Molière's *Don Juan*, brought out his *Libertine*, which was a new, but not an improved dramatic version of the Don Juan story; and as early as 1662, Sir Aston Cokain, in his tragedy of *Ovid*, published, but never acted, had turned to account the droll notion of asking a dead man to supper, and of the dead man's accepting the invitation and giving a banquet in return. Sir Aston

Cokain's profligate hero is a certain Captain Hannibal, who having, by the direction of a witch, cut a woman open and sewn up in her body a cat (!), takes refuge at Tomos, where he meets Ovid languishing in exile. After various adventures of a fantastic and revolting character, Captain Hannibal, and his servant Cacala, see on a gibbet the body of an executed criminal, and invite it to supper, even as Don Juan and Catalino (*alias* Arlecchino) had invited to supper the statue of the Commander. Captain Hannibal's sole reason for asking the corpse to supper is that—

" Some lying people
Repeat some of the dead have walked."

The final invitation is given and accepted in the following dialogue :—

" *Hannibal.*— If thou
Canst such a piece of fine activity show,
Come sup with me to-night ; thou shalt be wel-
come. [*Speaks to the hanged man.*]
" *Cacala.*—He bows his head.
" *Hannibal.*—Hang his head !'
" *Cacala.*—He need not put himself to such un-
necessary trouble
He that small favour hath received already."
&c. &c.

When the supper-hour arrives, the corpse, now described as a "Spectre," comes to the door and gives the

three knocks, which have since become traditional on the part of the statue of the Commander. Cacala, according to the stage direction, " opens the door, turns back, and falls down as in a swoon "; after which the Spectre enters. Hannibal begs him to sit down, and calls for Cacala :—

> "Cacala, where's Cacala? Give me a glass of
> wine. What! on the floor still? Rise, man!
> " *Cacala.*—I dare not stay, nor breathe, Sir.
> " *Hannibal.*—He will not hurt you!
> " *Spectre.*—I shall not be so rude when I find
> welcome,
> To do a mischief.
> " *Hannibal.*—Fill wine, Sir! Much good do
> you, and love's to you,
> To your fair mistresses' health, whether alive,
> Or your companion in the Elysian Groves!
> " *Spectre.*—You much endear me.
> " *Hannibal.*—Could I have thought you would
> have supped with me,
> You should have been much better treated.
> Sit down and eat, thou silly Cacala!"

Cacala is but a sorry imitation of that Italian Arlecchino, who, on the Statue's bowing to him, throws a somersault backwards, with a glass of wine in his hand, of which he does not spill a drop. Cacala, in a similar situation, " cries aloud, falls backward, and with his

legs under the table, overturns all the meat." For
Cacala to upset the meat must indeed have been much
easier than for Arlecchino not to spill the wine.

With the substitution of "the Spectre" for "the
Statue," the miraculous portion of the Don Juan
story is still followed in a sort of paraphrase. The
Spectre, as a matter of course, invites Captain Hannibal and Cacala to a return supper, which is given
"under the gibbet," and on a table covered with a
black cloth—an imitation of the table of black
marble on which Don Juan takes his supper in the
original Spanish play. During supper the Spectre
grows confidential, and tells Captain Hannibal how he
came to be executed. "The lords and gentry," he
commences, ("nobility and gentry" would not have
suited the rhythm) :—

> "The lords and gentry of
> This city Tomos gave orders to a statuary
> To make the image of the poet Ovid
> In beaten massy gold for the honour he
> Had done them by writing an excellent poem,
> In the Getick language, in Tiberius' praise.
> When it was ready to have been presented,
> I got into the house and stole it thence,
> Melted it privately and put it off
> By little parcels, spent it on wanton wenches
> And among boon companions; in my cups,
> Bragged on 't to two false brothers who betrayed
> me."

After listening to this long and improbable story, the Captain proposes to take his leave. But the Spectre tells him that he has provided "a little masque" for his entertainment; whereupon Œacus, Rhadamanthus, and Minos, the Judges of Hell, come in with Alecto, Sisyphone, and Megæra, the Furies. A dance takes place and is followed by this song :—

" Most happy is the libertine
And of mankind the most ingenious
Who from grave precepts doth decline
And doth indulge his jovial genius.
  Oh the joys, the joys
  They have that follow vice
  Without any fear of the gods,
  Who freely waste their treasures
  To purchase them their pleasures,
  And are with the virtuous at odds.

The atheist is the greatest fool
Who only aims to please his senses;
Thinking in heaven no gods bear rule,
  And tipples, murders, swears, and wenches.
  Oh the woes, the woes
  That follow all those
  Who wear out their lives in vice;
  That swear, kill, and drink,
  And never them bethink
  Till they fall into hell in a trice."

I.   8

"In a trice," sure enough, the gallant Captain is carried off by Judges and Furies combined; the Spectre exclaiming, as his late companion, not more vicious than himself, disappears :—

"Down the infernal shades
Of griefly Pluto's kingdom let him sink!
A fouler soul was never seen in hell
Where witchcraft, rapes, murders, and vicious life
Will find a suitable, endless punishment."

It says something for the intelligence of the manager of his time, that Sir Aston Cokain's play was never acted. It says something, also, for the folly of Sir Aston Cokain, that, being acquainted, as he evidently was, with either the Spanish or the Italian drama of *Don Juan*, or with both, he yet made so imperfect a use of them. The scenes borrowed from *Don Juan*, and spoilt in the borrowing, are employed episodically, and have no connection, except through the Spectre's story of the stolen statue, with the misfortunes of Ovid, which constitute the main subject of the piece. The work is interesting only as a literary curiosity, and as the first English drama in which the supernatural portion of the Don Juan drama is presented.

Shadwell's version of the Don Juan story is a most unsatisfactory affair. Instead of translating the *Burlador di Sevilla* of Tirso de Molina, or the *Convitato di Pietra* of Giliberti, or the *Festin de Pierre* of Molière, he took in hand an inferior work on the same subject by the French actor Rosimond—simply, it would seem, because he had chanced to see it played in Paris. Nor had he sense enough to reproduce Rosimond's drama as Rosimond had written it. He had his own little pride as an adapter, and altered Rosimond's play in many places merely for the sake of alteration.

Shadwell fell into one very absurd mistake. Rosimond, unable to account to himself for the title "Festin de Pierre" by which the Don Juan piece had already in several versions become known to the French public, imagined that the name of the Commander invited to the "festin" must have been "Pierre," and took upon himself so to baptize him. But it struck the ingenious Shadwell that the Commander, having been a Spaniard, must have been called not "Pierre" but "Pedro." Thus in its passage through French into English, "the Guest of Stone" became converted into "The Banquet of Don Pedro." Shadwell, however, assuming that the Commander must have had something to command, named him Commander or Commandant. But Don Gonzalo de Ulloa was only a commander in a military order. Had he been the chief of the military force in Seville, it is absurd to suppose that Don Juan could have killed him and still gone about unmolested. In fact,

Don Juan was, by his family and by the influence of his father, a much more important personage than the retired officer whom he slew in single combat after behaving outrageously to his daughter.

One unfortunate effect of Shadwell's monstrously melo-dramatic rendering of the Don Juan story has been that no fair version of Tirso de Molina's famous play has ever been brought out in this country. A French translation of " El Burlador di Sevilla " may be found in M. Alphonse Royer's " Théâtre de Tirso de Molina"; and although M. Royer thinks the work deficient in unity, it is at least more natural and more life-like than most other dramas on the same well-worked theme. The characters of the original play possess a reality which scarcely belongs to the somewhat abstract personages of the opera. The different moods of the lively and coquettish Zerlina, the elegant and sentimental Elvira, the passionate Anna, are, no doubt, admirably expressed by the music. But some of the prime agents in the drama, including Elvira and Don Juan himself, are absolutely without belongings. They might have dropped from the clouds. Elvira, it may be said, is Don Juan's wife. But so were a thousand other women—or, to be exact, one thousand and two.

Don Juan's relations to Donna Anna, and through Donna Anna to the Commander, are brought out clearly and forcibly enough. Zerlina, too, possesses reality; which does not alter the fact that her adventures with Don Juan are quite episodical and have no visible connection with the general progress of the drama. But the most inexplicable personage of the whole piece is Don Juan himself. No one knows whence he comes nor whither he goes; and, meanwhile, whatever crimes he may commit, no official notice is taken of them. His freedom from punishment is accounted for in Tirso de Molina's play by the high position of his father. The law has been put in action against him; but the powerful officials, his father's friends, will not allow him to be touched; and, precisely as in the old chronicle, on which the legend itself would seem to be founded, family influence enables him, practically, to break the law with impunity. It is known that in the "Chronicle of Seville" Don Juan is said to have been put to death by Franciscan monks who enticed him into their convent and, after punishing the scoffer, spread the report that his contempt for the mystery of death, and his insult to the divine powers—*crimen læsæ majestatis divinæ*— had drawn down upon him direct vengeance from above.

In Mozart's opera, however, there is neither father, nor King, nor judges, nor magistrates, nor police; justice being administered in the operatic Seville either by stone statues or not at all. Contrary indeed to the usual historical course, the theme treated realistically

by Tirso de Molina, lost after the lapse of a century
and a half all trace of reality to acquire, as treated by
Mozart, a purely symbolical character. Tirso de Molina's
play is the anecdote of the "Chronicle of Seville"
dramatised. Mozart's opera presents the essential
features of the story, but stripped of those surroundings and adjuncts which in Tirso de Molina's work
give the incidents (apart, of course, from the miraculous ones) a look of actual probability. Seeing the
Don Juan of Mozart, it would occur to no one that the
subject could have been taken from real life; and
Hoffmann, going a step beyond Mozart, and transport-
ing it still further into the regions of the ideal, gives
to it such symbolical significance as anyone may find
for himself in *Tannhäuser* and *Lohengrin*, but which
it required the poetical vision of Hoffman to discover
in Mozart's *Don Giovanni*.

CHAPTER XIII.

MOZART'S "DON JUAN" DESCRIBED BY HOFFMAN.

THE large theatre was tastefully decorated and magnificently lighted. The pit and boxes were crowded. The first notes of the overture convinced me that the orchestra was excellent, and I remained in expectation of all the pleasures which a masterpiece can afford. At the very first notes of the *andante* the terrors of the awful subterranean *regno del pianto* took possession of me, and dread entered into my soul. The joyous flourish in the seventh bar of the *allegro* re-echoed like a criminal's shouts of pleasure. I fancied I could see threatening demons emerging from the darkness of hell, and forms animated by gaiety madly dancing on the thin covering of a bottomless abyss. The conflict between human nature and the unknown enjoyments which surround it for its destruction presented itself clearly before my mind. At last the curtain rose, the storm had ceased.

Half frozen in his thick cloak, and in a very bad temper, Leporello is keeping watch under the pavilion, in the darkness of the night, and begins *"Notte e giorno faticar."* "So it is to be in Italian," I say to myself. *Ah! che piacere!* then I shall hear all the airs and all the recitatives just as the great master conceived them in his mind and just as he has transmitted them to us! Don Juan rushes on the stage, and behind him, Donna Anna, holding back the wrongdoer by his cloak. What a noble bearing! what a head! eyes which shoot forth electric sparks of love, hatred, anger, despair! Ringlets of black hair wave over her dark Andalusian neck; that loose white drapery at the same moment covers and betrays charms which none have looked on without peril. Still agitated, her bosom falls and heaves with the violence of her emotion. And what a voice she has! Hear her sing, *"Non sperar se non m'uccidi!"* Amid the tumultuous music of the orchestra, like flashes of lightning in a storm, are heard the fiendish words of Don Juan in vain striving to get free. Does he really wish to liberate himself? Why does he not violently push off this weak woman? Why does he not take flight? Can it be [that the crime he has just committed has shattered his strength; or is it the struggle between love and hate raging within him that steals away his courage? The aged father has paid the penalty of his madness with his life, for truly madness was it to fight in the darkness of night against so terrible a foe. Don Juan and Leporello come forward. Don Juan takes off his brown cloak and remains in a costume of red satin, richly embroidered. A strong and noble form! His face is manly, his eyes piercing, his lips gently rounded. The extraordinary play of the muscles of his forehead gives him a diabolical expression, which causes a slight fear without diminishing the beauty of his features. One would say that he could fascinate at will, that women when once they have been subjected to the magic of his glance could no longer get free, but would be obliged to accomplish their perdition of their own accord.

Long and lanky, wearing a red and white striped waistcoat, a little grey cloak, and a white hat with a red feather, Leporello stalks upon the boards. His features present an odd mixture of good humour, sharpness, irony, and joviality. One can see at a glance that the old rascal is just suited to be the servant and accomplice of Don Juan. They have safely scaled the wall and escaped. Torches are brought in. Donna Anna reappears, followed by Ottavio, a little dandy, neat and formal in his dress, and one-and-twenty at the most. He is engaged to Anna and probably lives in the house. Otherwise, how could he have been called so quickly? He heard the noise at first, and might, perhaps, if he had hurried, have saved her father. But the little beau could not come without finishing his toilet, and he was afraid of catching cold from the night air. There is more than the expression, of mere despair at the dreadful event in the sounds of the duet and of those recitatives, to which the wailing of flutes and hautboys gives such precious artificial aid.

Donna Elvira, still showing traces of great beauty, but of a beauty which has begun to fade, comes to complain of Don Juan's treachery; and Leporello, with much sympathy and ready wit, was remarking that she spoke like a book—*parla come un libro stampato* —when I fancied I could hear someone behind me. Anyone might easily have opened the door and sat down in the back part of the box. I felt more than usually annoyed. I was so pleased to be alone in the box, listening at ease to such an excellent performance of a divine masterpiece ; to let myself be carried away by the impressions it afforded, and to yield myself up entirely to myself! A single stupid word would have cruelly torn me away from my enthusiasm. I resolved to pay no attention to my neighbour, but devote myself entirely to the performance ; to avoid every word, every look. I rested my head on my hand, turned my back to my companion,

and my eyes to the stage. The whole representation
fully carried out the promise of the opening scene.
Little Zerlina, loving and sprightly, was consoling
that poor fool Masetto, with her charming, coaxing
ways. Don Juan was pouring out his contempt for
such people who served but as tools to aid his pleasures,
in the brusque and impetuous air, "*Finch' han del
vino.*" The play of his features gave admirably the
expression of his thought. The three maskers appeared.
Their prayer rose in pure strains to heaven. The back
of the theatre was laid open. Shouts of joy, mingled
with the clinking of glasses, resound. The peasants
and all the maskers, attracted by the Governor's feast,
were dancing and forming themselves into animated
groups. The three conspirators, bound by an oath to
take vengeance on Juan, arrive. A solemn stillness
seizes upon the revellers. Then the dance begins again
and continues until the rescue of Zerlina. Don Juan
advances boldly with drawn sword against his enemy,
disarms him, and forces his way through the crowd of
terrified peasants.

I had, for some time, fancied I could hear a fresh
and delicate breathing just behind me, and a sound
like the rustling of a silk dress. I suspected that a
lady was in the box. But deeply immersed in the
imaginary world which the music opened to my view,
I did not suffer my dreams to be disturbed. . . . . No
words can express my astonishment. Donna Anna,

dressed just as I had seen her on the stage, was there,
gazing at me with eyes brimful of soul and of expression. I remained speechless and looked at her
in a terror of surprise. Her mouth (at least, so I
fancied) formed a slightly ironical smile, in which I
thought I saw the reflection of my stupid face. I felt
I must speak to her, and yet surprise—I will not say
fright—weighed upon my tongue and made it motionless. At last these words involuntarily escaped me,
"How is it, Madam, that I see you here?" She
answered me, in the purest Tuscan, that if I did not
understand Italian she would be deprived of the pleasure of my conversation, for this was the only language
which she spoke or understood. Her words were very
soft, and sounded like a song. As she spoke, her eyes,
which were of dark blue, gained in expression, and
each glance from them made my heart beat. It was
Donna Anna, without the least doubt. I never thought
of questioning the possibility of her double presence
in the body of the theatre and upon the stage. With
what pleasure would I repeat my conversation with the
Signora; but when I translate it, each word seems
stiff and pale; every phrase seems too heavy to
represent the grace and lightness of the Tuscan
idiom.

While she spoke of *Don Juan,* and of her part, it seemed
to me that all the secret treasures of this masterpiece
were laid before me, and that for the first time I

entered into an unknown world. She told me that music was her whole life, and that often, while she sang, she seemed to understand many a meaning which till then had been lying unintelligible in her heart. " Yes, I understand everything then," she said, her sparkling eyes adding to the animation of her voice; " but all lies cold and dead around me, when, instead of understanding me—of guessing my meaning—they applaud me for some brilliant and difficult performance or for some graceful *fioriture*. Then a hand of iron seems to close upon my heart! But you, you understand me, for I know that the empire of the imagination and the marvellous, in which heavenly sensations are to be found, is open to you also ! "

" What! heavenly being—then, you know . . . ? "

She smiled and pronounced my name.

The bell rang; a sudden paleness replaced the natural colour of her cheeks. Donna Anna put her hand to her heart, as if a sudden pain had seized upon her, and said in a low voice: " Poor Anna ! thy most terrible moments are at hand." She vanished from the box.

The first act had filled me with transports of delight; it was ravishing. But after this miraculous incident the music had upon me a different though no less striking and powerful effect. It was, as it were, the long-looked-for accomplishment of my most secret presentiments. In the scene with Donna Anna I felt

myself carried away by a voluptuous atmosphere which
gently rocked me as in a cradle. My eyes shut against
my will. I felt, as it were, a kiss upon my lips, but
this kiss had all the intangibility and duration of the
most melodious sound.

"*Già la mensa è preparata.*" This finale was executed with the most disorderly glee. Seated at a
table and flirting with two girls, Don Juan was making
champagne corks pop one after another, and giving
freedom to the wild spirits which bubbled impatiently
at their restraint. The room, not a very spacious one,
ended in a high Gothic window, through which the
clouds of evening could be seen. Even while Elvira
was reminding the faithless Juan of all his broken
vows, lightning was seen to shoot along the sky, and
the dull sound of thunder in the distance gave signs
of the approaching storm. At last a violent knocking
is heard at the door. Elvira and the two girls take
refuge in flight, and amid the fearful music of demons,
sounding the alarm, the colossus of stone stalks in.
Don Juan looks a pigmy at its side, and the ground
trembles under the thundering footsteps of the giant.

Amid the tempest, the thunder, and the fearful
cries of the demons, Don Juan, atheist to the last,
pronounces with a firm voice his terrible "No!"
The knell of his destruction has sounded. The statue
disappears and a thick vapour fills the theatre. Gradually it disperses and reveals an awful sight. Don

Juan is tossing amid the torments of hell, and is seen only from time to time amid the crowd of fiends. Suddenly a frightful explosion occurs. Don Juan with the band of fiends has disappeared, and Leporello lies motionless at full length in a corner of the stage.

A sort of general praise was accorded to the actors and the well-known beauty of their singing; but some little sarcastic observations, thrown in here and there, proved to me that none of the critics had even a suspicion of the deep and sublime aim of this opera of operas ! *oper der opern !*

Now I am more master of my feelings, and find myself able, my dear Theodore, to point out to you what I thought I saw in this admirable work of the divine Mozart.

Only the poet understands the poet. The soul must have been consecrated in the temple to guess unaided those mysteries which remain unintelligible to the uninitiated. If we consider the poem of Don Juan, without seeking for its inmost thought, if we see in it only the fable on which it was constructed by Da Ponte, we can scarcely understand how Mozart conceived and composed so beautiful an opera from such a plot. A dissolute fellow, unreasonably given to wine and women, who madly invites to his table the statue of an old man whom he killed in defence of his own life:—truly there is not much poetry in that, and we must agree that such a man is hardly

worth the trouble taken by the infernal powers in
coming on earth to fetch him. He does not deserve
that a stone statue should take to itself a soul and
come down on purpose from its marble horse to warn
him of the wrath of heaven; and that, besides all
this, thunder should growl and lightning flash for him.

Believe me, Theodore, when I say that nature provided Don Juan, as the dearest of her children, with
everything which can elevate a man above the common
herd whose lot is misery and toil. She was prodigal
to him of all the gifts which bring humanity near to
the essence of the divine. She destined him to shine,
to conquer, to rule. She gave a noble organisation to
his powerful and well-made frame. Into his breast
she dropped a spark of heavenly flame. He had a
lofty soul, a quick and lively understanding. But it is
the dreadful consequence of our origin that the enemy
of our race has retained the power of consuming a man
by the man himself, by giving him that desire of the
infinite, that thirst for what he can never obtain. This
conflict of God with the devil is the struggle between
moral and material life.

The desires of which Don Juan's powerful organisation was the mother made him drunk; a constant
ardour made his blood boil, and led him continually to
sensual pleasures in hope of obtaining a satisfaction
which he always sought in vain.

Nothing on earth elevates a man more in his inmost

thoughts than love. It is love whose powerful and victorious influence brightens our heart, and fills it at
the same moment with happiness and confusion. Can
we wonder that Don Juan hoped to appease by love
the desires which tore his breast, and that the devil
thus entrapped him? It is he who inspired Don Juan
with the thought that by love of woman we can fulfil
those divine promises which we carry inscribed in the
depths of our soul. Infinite desire, which from the
first day proves our kinship with the divine! Flying
from one beauty to another, enjoying their charms
even to satiety, even to the most overpowering intoxication; ever deeming himself deceived in his choice, and
ever hoping to attain the ideal he pursued, Don Juan
found himself at last choked by the pleasures of
this life; and looking with contempt upon mankind,
how could he fail to hate those phantoms of pleasure
which he had long regarded as the greatest prize of
life, and which had turned out such a cruel mockery
for him? Every woman whom he injured was no
longer a joy of the senses for him, but an audacious
insult alike to human nature and to her Creator. A
deep disdain for the common way of looking at that
life above whose level he felt that he was raised; an
ironical and never-ending sense of amusement which
he felt on looking at the so-called happiness of those
beneath him; the contempt inspired by the quiet and
peacefulness of those who had never felt the need of

carrying out the high destinies of our divine nature—
all these feelings led him to make a cruel sport of these
gentle, humble, plaintive creatures, and treat them as
marks for the sallies of his worn-out nature. Every
time he shattered the peace of a united family or
carried off from her lover a cherished bride, it was
for him a triumph over human nature and God. His
abduction of Anna, with the circumstances accompanying it, is the greatest of these victories to which
he can lay claim.

Donna Anna is contrasted with Don Juan by the
great perfection with which she also has been endowed.
She as well as Don Juan has had beauty both of body
and soul for her portion; but she has retained purity
and her ideal candour, so that hell can only destroy her
upon earth. As soon as this crime is accomplished,
vengeance must come. Donna Anna was made to be
Don Juan's ideal, to rescue him from that despair to
which he falls a victim through his fatal passions. But
he beheld her too late, and can only accomplish the
diabolical thought of her perdition. She is not saved.
She falls! For when Don Juan appears at the beginning of the first act he has gained his end. The devilish
fire which burns in his soul has rendered all resistance
useless. Only he, Don Juan alone, could excite in her
that mad delight which brings her to his arms. After
her fall all the disastrous consequences of her fault
occur at once. The death of her father, slain by the

hand of Don Juan; her engagement to the cold,
common-place, effeminate Don Ottavio, whom she once
thought she loved; even that love which consumes her,
which scorched her bosom from the first instant that
she yielded to it, all makes her feel that the destruction
of Don Juan can alone give her back repose; but this
repose will be death for her. We see her, then, cease-
lessly urging on her frigid lover to revenge; she herself pursues the betrayer; and it is not until she has
seen him suffer the torments of divine vengeance that
calm re-enters her breast. But she will never yield
to this betrothed husband who is always ready to get
married :

> " Lascia, o caro, un anno ancora,"
> &c. &c. &c.

But she will never outlive this year. Don Ottavio will
never behold in his arms the woman on whom Don
Juan has left the burning imprints of his passion.

9 *

CHAPTER XIV.

ALFRED DE MUSSET'S "DON JUAN."

WHEN a poet criticises he does not pull to pieces the work which he has undertaken to explain; he reproduces its spirit in another and more palpable form. Hoffman did this in the case of *Don Giovanni;* and his criticism—if criticism it is to be called—has had the effect of stamping his idea of Don Juan upon the mind of more than one poet who was afterwards to deal with the same suggestive subject. After Tirso de Molina, Giliberti, Molière, Gluck, Mozart, and Byron, the fertile theme was yet to be handled by Alfred de Musset and by the Russian poet Poushkin. Alfred de Musset, in adopting Hoffman's type, does the great national dramatist of France the injustice of condemning the much more real Don Juan of *Le Festin de Pierre.*

Let him, however, speak for himself in his own beautiful language* :—

Quant au roué français, au don Juan ordinaire,
Ivre, riche, joyeux, raillant l'homme de pierre,
Ne demandant partout qu'à trouver le vin bon,
Bernant monsieur Dimanche, et disant à son père
Qu'il serait mieux assis pour lui faire un sermon,
C'est l'ombre d'un roué qui ne vaut pas Valmont.

Il en est un plus grand, plus beau, plus poétique,
Que personne n'a fait, que Mozart a rêvé,
Qu'Hoffmann a vu passer, au son de la musique,
Sous un éclair divin de sa nuit fantastique,
Admirable portrait qu'il n'a point achevé,
Et que de notre temps Shakspeare aurait trouvé.

Un jeune homme est assis au bord d'une prairie,
Pensif comme l'amour, beau comme le génie ;
Sa maîtresse enivrée est prête à s'endormir.
Il vient d'avoir vingt ans, son cœur vient de s'ouvrir ;
Rameau tremblant encor de l'arbre de la vie,
Tombé, comme le Christ, pour aimer et souffrir.

Le voilà se noyant dans des larmes de femme
Devant cette nature aussi belle que lui ;
Pressant le monde entier sur son cœur qui se pâme,
Faible, et, comme le lierre, ayant besoin d'autrui ;
Et ne se cachant pas, et suspendant son ame,
Comme un luth éolien, aux lèvres de la nuit.

---

* From "un Spectacle dans un Fauteuil."

Le voilà demandant pourquoi son cœur soupire,
Jurant, les yeux en pleurs, qu'il ne désire rien ;
Caressant sa maîtresse, et des sons de sa lyre
Égayant son sommeil comme un ange gardien ;
Tendant sa coupe d'or à ceux qu'il voit sourire,
Voulant voir leur bonheur pour y chercher le sien.

Le voilà, jeune et beau, sous le ciel de la **France**,
Déjà riche à vingt ans comme un enfouisseur ;
Portant sur la nature un cœur plein d'espérance,
Aimant, aimé de tous, ouvert comme une fleur ;
Si candide et si frais que l'ange d'innocence
Baiserait sur son front la beauté de son cœur.

Le voilà, regardez, devinez-lui sa vie.
Quel sort peut-on prédire à cet enfant du ciel ?
L'amour en l'approchant jure d'être éternel ;
Le hasard pense à lui,—la sainte Poésie
Retourne en souriant sa coupe d'ambroisie
Sur ses cheveux plus doux et plus blonds que le miel.

Ce palais, c'est le sien ; le serf et la campagne
Sont à lui ;—la forêt, le fleuve et la montagne
Ont retenu son nom en écoutant l'écho.
C'est à lui le village, et le pâle troupeau
Des moines.—Quand il passe et traverse un hameau,
Le bon ange du lieu se lève et l'accompagne.

Quatre filles de prince ont demandé sa main.
Sachez que s'il voulait la reine pour maîtresse,
Et trois palais de plus, il les aurait demain ;
Qu'un juif deviendrait chauve à compter sa richesse,
Et qu'il pourrait jeter, sans que rien en paraisse,
Les blés de ses moissons aux oiseaux du chemin.

Eh bien ! cet homme-là vivra dans les tavernes
Entre deux charbonniers autour d'un poêle assis ;
La poudre noircira sa barbe et ses sourcils ;
Vous le verrez un jour, tremblant et les yeux ternes,
Venir dans son manteau dormir sous les lanternes,
La face ensanglantée et les coudes noircis.

Vous le verrez sauter sur l'échelle dorée,
Pour courir dans un bouge au sortir d'un boudoir,
Portant sa lèvre ardente à la prostituée,
Avant qu'à son balcon donc Elvire éplorée,
Dans la profonde nuit croyant encor le voir,
Ait cessé d'agiter sa lampe et son mouchoir.

Vous le verrez, laquais pour une chambrière,
Cachant sous ses habits son valet grelottant ;
Vous le verrez, tranquille et froid comme une pierre,
Pousser dans le ruisseau le cadavre d'un père,
Et laisser le vieillard traîner ses mains de sang
Sur des murs chauds encor du viol de son enfant.

Que direz-vous alors ? Ah ! vous croirez peut-être
Que le monde a blessé ce cœur vaste et hautain,
Que c'est quelque Lara qui se sent méconnaître,
Que l'homme a mal jugé, qui sait ce qu'il peut être,
Et qui, s'apercevant qu'il le serait en vain,
Rend haine contre haine et dédain pour dédain.

Eh bien ! vous vous trompez.—Jamais personne au monde
N'a pensé moins que lui qu'il était oublié.
Jamais il n'a frappé sans qu'on ne lui réponde ;
Jamais il n'a senti l'inconstance de l'onde,
Et jamais il n'a vu se dresser sous son pié
Le vivace serpent de la fausse amitié.

Que dis-je ? tel qu'il est, le monde l'aime encore ;
Il n'a perdu chez lui ni ses biens ni son rang.
Devant Dieu, devant tous, il s'asseoit à son banc.
Ce qu'il a fait de mal, personne ne l'ignore ;
On connaît son génie, on l'admire, on l'honore—
—Seulement, voyez-vous, cet homme, c'est don Juan.

Oui, don Juan.   Le voilà ce nom que tout répète,
Ce nom mystérieux que tou l'univers prend,
Dont chacun vient parler et que nul ne comprend ;
Si vaste et si puissant qu'il n'est pas de poète
Qui ne l'ait soulevé dans son cœur et sa tête,
Et pour l'avoir tenté ne soit resté plus grand.

Insensé que je suis ! que fais je ici moi-même ?
E'tait-ce donc mon tour de leur parler de toi,
Grande ombre, et d'où viens-tu pour tomber jusqu'à moi ?
C'est qu'avec leurs horreurs, leur doute et leur blasphème,
Pas un d'eux ne t'aimait, don Juan ; et moi je t'aime,
Comme le vieux Blondel aimait son pauvre roi.

Oh ! qui me jettera sur ton coursier rapide !
Et qui me prêtera le manteau voyageur,
Pour te suivre en pleurant, candide corrupteur !
Qui me déroulera cette liste homicide,
Cette liste d'amour si remplie et si vide,
Et que ta main peuplait des oublis de ton cœur !

Trois mille noms charmants ! trois mille noms de femme !
Pas un qu'avec des pleurs tu n'ais balbutié !
Et ce foyer d'amour qui dévorait ton ame,
Qui, lorsque tu mourus, de tes veines de flamme
Remonta dans le ciel comme un ange oublié,
De ces trois mille amours pas un qui l'ait noyé !

Elles t'aimaient pourtant, ces filles insensées
Que sur ton cœur de fer tu pressas tour à tour !
Le vent qui t'emportait les avait traversées ;
Elles t'aimaient, don Juan, ces pauvres délaissées
Qui couvraient de baisers l'ombre de ton amour,
Qui te donnaient leur vie, et qui n'avaient qu'un jour !

Mais toi, spectre énervé, toi, que faisais-tu d'elles ?
Ah ! massacre et malheur, tu les aimais aussi !
Toi, croyant toujours voir sur tes amours nouvelles
Se lever le soleil de tes nuits éternelles,
Te disant chaque soir : Peut-être le voici,
Et l'attendant toujours, et vieillissant ainsi !

Demandant aux forêts, à la mer, à la plaine,
Aux brises du matin, à toute heure, à tout lieu,
La femme de ton ame et de ton premier vœu !
Prenant pour fiancée un rêve, une ombre vaine,
Et fouillant dans le cœur d'une hécatombe humaine,
Prêtre désespéré pour y chercher ton dieu.

Et que voulais-tu donc ?—Voilà ce que le monde
Au bout de trois cents ans demande encor tout bas.
Le sphinx aux yeux perçants attend qu'on lui réponde.
Ils savent compter l'heure, et que leur terre est ronde,
Ils marchent dans leur ciel sur le bout d'un compas,
Mais ce que tu voulais, ils ne le savent pas.

" Quelle est donc, disent-ils, cette femme inconnue,
    Qui seule eût mis la main au frein de son coursier ?
Qu'il appelait toujours et qui n'est pas venue ?
Où l'avait-il trouvée ? Où l'avait-il perdue ? .
Et quel nœud si puissant avait su les lier,
Que n'ayant pu venir, il n'ait pu l'oublier ?

" N'en était-il pas une, ou plus noble, ou plus belle,
Parmi tant de beautés, qui, de loin ou de près,
De son vague idéal eût du moins quelques traits ?
Que ne la gardait-il ? qu'on nous dise laquelle."
Toutes lui ressemblaient,—ce n'était jamais elle ;
Toutes lui ressemblaient, don Juan, et tu marchais !

Tu ne t'es pas lassé de parcourir la terre !
Ce vain fantôme, à qui Dieu t'avait envoyé !
Tu n'en as pas brisé la forme sous ton pié !
Tu n'es pas remonté, comme l'aigle à son aire
Sans avoir sa pature, ou comme le tonnerre
Dans sa nue aux flancs d'or, sans avoir foudroyé !

Tu n'as médit jamais de ce monde stupide
Qui te dévisageait d'un regard d'hébété ;
Tu l'as vu, tel qu'il est, dans sa difformité ;
Et tu montais toujours cette montagne aride,
Et tu suçais toujours, plus jeune et plus avide,
Les mamelles d'airain de la Réalité.

Et la vierge aux yeux bleus, sur la souple ottomane,
Dans ses bras parfumés te berçait mollement ;
De la fille du roi jusqu'à la paysanne
Tu ne méprisais rien, même la courtisane,
A qui tu disputais son misérable amant ;
Mineur, qui dans un puits cherchais un diamant.

Tu parcourais Madrid, Paris, Naple et Florence :
Grand seigneur aux palais, voleur aux carrefours ;
Ne comptant ni l'argent, ni les nuits, ni les jours ;
Apprenant du passant à chanter la romance ;
Ne demandant à Dieu, pour aimer l'existence,
Que ton large horizon et tes larges amours.

Tu retrouvais partout la vérité hideuse,
Jamais ce qu'ici-bas cherchaient tes vœux ardents,
Partout l'hydre éternel qui te montrait les dents;
Et poursuivant toujours ta vie aventureuse, ,
Regardant sous tes pieds cette mer orageuse,
Tu te disais tout bas : Ma perte est là-dedans.

Tu mourus plein d'espoir dans ta route infinie,
Et te souciant peu de laisser ici-bas
Des larmes et du sang aux traces de tes pas.
Plus vaste que le ciel et plus grand que la vie,
Tu perdis ta beauté, ta gloire et ton génie,
Pour un être impossible et qui n'existait pas.

Et le jour que parut le convive de pierre,
Tu vins à sa rencontre, et lui tendis la main ;
Tu tombas foudroyé sur ton dernier festin :
Symbole merveilleux de l'homme sur la terre,
Cherchant de ta main gauche à soulever ton verre,
Abandonnant ta droite à celle du Destin !

Maintenant, c'est à toi, lecteur, de reconnaître
Dans quel gouffre sans fond peut descendre ici-bas
Le rêveur insensé qui voudrait d'un tel maître.
Je ne dirai qu'un mot, et tu le comprendras :
Ce que don Juan aimait, Hassan l'aimait peut-être ;
Ce que don Juan cherchait, Hassan n'y croyait pas.

CHAPTER XV.

POUSHKIN'S ADDITIONAL SCENE FOR "FAUST" AND
NEW LAST ACT FOR "DON JUAN."

LYRIC poets would be scarcely human if, instead of
confining themselves to the exercise of their own
special faculty, they did not, from time to time, write
plays. Accordingly Byron in England, Alfred de
Musset in France, and Poushkin in Russia, all published dramas, of which the fate, as connected with the
stage, was different in each country. Our managers
seized on "Sardanapalus" in spite of Byron's protest
that the work was not intended for representation, and
that he would not on any account allow it to be played.
Byron objected to the chance of being "damned," and
was not anxious for the approbation of a mixed
theatrical audience, whose opinion he held to be far

less valuable than that of his ordinary reading public. To show that desire for applause had no necessary correlation with fear of hisses, he pointed out that, though he disliked being stung by a wasp, he did not for that reason admire the insect's hum; and that painful as the kick of a donkey might be, he could yet derive no pleasure from the animal's bray. Our laws in respect to literary property were less effective in Byron's time than they are now, when, though novelists may be plundered at will by playwrights in combination with managers, the principle is at least recognised that a drama is the property of the dramatist who writes it.

Alfred de Musset, when he gave his "Comedies and Proverbs" to the world in printed volumes, could scarcely have meant it to be understood that these works were but continuations of his "Spectacle dans un Fauteuil." In writing them he thought, no doubt, of readers first and of possible spectators afterwards, if at all. Some ingenious persons have suggested that if Alfred de Musset did not go to the managers with his plays, he adopted that course as the surest way of making the managers come to him. This theory, however, is contradicted by a certain number of facts. Musset published his minor dramatic works one by one, as he wrote them, in literary periodicals; and they were all produced at a theatre when it might fairly be assured that the majority of the audience were already

acquainted with them in their printed form. There
can be no question as to Poushkin's not having
intended his dramatic works for representation. In
France, with more cultivated audiences, a piece of high
literary work in dramatic form may, however unsuited
to the stage, succeed by literary worth alone, as so many
of Alfred de Musset's have succeeded. In England
our managers have often been enterprising enough to
give a dramatic poem a fair chance, even in cases where
the poet would rather have been excused. But owing
either to the inferiority of our actors, or to the lower
level of our theatrical audiences, or from both causes,
such experiments have never yet obtained more than a
partial and temporary success. In Russia a literary
drama of the kind sometimes described as "more fit
for the closet than the stage" would be less likely to
please the public than in England—far less likely than
in France; and the dramatic works published by the
greatest of Russian poets have never had their essential
dramatic value tested by being represented on the
boards. Indeed, the three most interesting (so far as
foreign readers are concerned) of Poushkin's compositions in dialogue, have more the character of psycho-
logical studies than of stage-plays. One deals with
the supposed poisoning of Mozart by Salieri; another
with the condition of Faust after the loss of Margaret;
a third with the fate of Don Juan, who in Poushkin's
sketch perishes, of course, by the traditional agency of

the " Stone Guest," but differs from the Don Juan of
previous dramatists through being seriously in love
with his principal victim.

If Salieri did not poison Mozart, as was at one
time believed, it is quite certain that Mozart poisoned
the existence of Salieri, who could not endure the
superiority of his rival. Mozart's success need not of
itself have pained him, for it was often contested.
The Marriage of Figaro was hissed at Vienna; a fact
of which Mozart himself made a note in the supper
scene of *Don Giovanni*, where Leporello, hearing his
master's private orchestra play, among other operatic
tunes of the day, " Non piu andriai," exclaims, with a
shake of the head, "Ah, we know that only too well!"
Salieri also knew "only too well" the opera of which
the cited air was intended to remind the public. He
knew it to be a masterpiece, and hated its composer,
not, as some writers have imagined, because he could
not appreciate Mozart's music, but because he regarded
it as unapproachable. This, at least, is Poushkin's
idea—an idea which his countryman Oulibicheff afterwards developed in one of the finest passages of his "Life
of Mozart." *Don Giovanni*, it must be remembered,
was eclipsed at Vienna by one of Salieri's works, as the
Marriage of Figaro had previously been eclipsed by
Martini's *Cosa rara*—the work from which Don Juan's
musicians borrow the pretty melody in 6-8 time in the
before-mentioned supper scene. " I leave to psycho-

logists," says Oulibicheff, " the task of deciding whether
the day on which Salieri triumphed publicly over
Mozart was the happiest or the most miserable of his
life. · He did, indeed, triumph, thanks to the ignorance
of the Viennese, to his own talents as a director, which
had enabled him to render the work of his rival scarcely
recognizable, and to the devotion of his subordinates.
He ought to have been content in all respects; but
Salieri was not only envious, he was also a great musician. He had read the score of *Don Giovanni*, and
you know that the works a man reads with the greatest
attention are those of his enemies. With what
desperate admiration this study must have filled the
soul of an artist more ambitious of true glory than of
mere success! How he must have judged himself in
his secret heart! What serpents must have writhed
and hissed in the laurel wreath that had just been
placed on his brow ! "

Painfully impressed by a sense of his own hopeless
inferiority, the Salieri of Poushkin's dramatic sketch,
seeks to justify his hatred of Mozart by exaggerating
to himself Mozart's careless and almost reckless mode
of life. Gluck's favourite pupil is represented as
striving in vain to produce, as a result of systematic
study, what the composer of the *Marriage of Figaro* is
able to dash off at a moment's notice in a tavern amid
the click of billiard balls, or at home the night
before the piece which occupies him is to be executed,

drinking glass after glass of hot punch. Mozart, with all his facility and all his power, does not, according to Salieri, respect the dignity of art ; and the comparatively impotent composer is sincerely shocked when the great musical inventor brings with him into a wine-cellar a street player who has amused him by burlesquing one of his most beautiful melodies on the violin.

Without being a faithful reproduction of the man, this figure may have been suggested to Poushkin by that of Copanek, who, though only an itinerant musician, became for a time Mozart's friend, and who, at least, played well enough to induce Mozart to compose a melody expressly for him. Salieri, gloomy egotist as he is, cannot forgive Mozart his gaiety and generosity. He somehow persuades himself that his rival, with all his inspiration, has done nothing to advance the science of music; and partly for this reason, but principally because he loathes the composer of so many masterpieces, he takes an opportunity of giving him a dose of peculiar poison, which he had kept for twenty years, often tempted to administer it, but never yielding to the temptation, because never quite convinced until now that he had before him a man whom he detested more than he could possibly detest anyone else.

In the picture of Faust as he might have been after the death of Margaret, and after the gratification,

I. 10

through Mephistopheles, of an immense number of wishes, we find that person suffering a little from remorse and a great deal from ennui. He has become cruel, moreover, and, simply to relieve the dull monotony of life, and in order that something may happen, orders the obedient fiend to sink a large West Indiaman, "laden with chocolate, gold, three hundred passengers, and two monkeys."

Tht "Guest of Stone" was never meant for publication even in book form. Found among the writer's papers after his death in 1837, it bears the date of 1830; so that Poushkin, before producing it, might have read Hoffman's "Vision of Don Juan," in which, as in the Russian poet's new last act, Donna Anna is supposed to be in love with her would-be seducer. In Poushkin's "Guest of Stone," however, this idea is improved upon; for Don Juan is, on his side, represented as seriously and profoundly in love with Donna Anna. Hoffman had, indeed, described Donna Anna as that ideal which Don Juan had always been in search of, but which he was destined not to find until he had already rendered himself unworthy of it and unable any longer to appreciate it. "Donna Anna," wrote Hoffman, "was made to be Don Juan's ideal, to snatch him from that despair which inspired him with such fatal ardours; but, seeing her too late, he could only conceive the diabolical thought of ruining her." In Poushkin's new last act to *Don Juan*, Donna

Anna is represented not as the daughter but as the young wife of the venerable Commander. Don Juan had slain the old gentleman at the proper time and now hears from a monk that the inconsolable widow prays daily at her husband's tomb. There in monk's disguise Don Juan arrives, makes himself known to Donna Anna, tells in burning language the story of his love, and at last obtains from her a promise to visit him that evening. No sooner does Don Juan find himself alone with the Commander's statue than he invites it, not to sup with him, but to keep watch outside his apartment during Donna Anna's visit. The statue accepts; but instead of waiting outside, comes in, interrupts Don Juan in the midst of a passionate appeal to Donna Anna, and ends in the usual manner by carrying him down to the place of eternal torments.

Poushkin's Don Juan dies game, like all other Don Juans, except, indeed, the first of all; for in Tirso de Molina's play the profligate hero calls for a priest, and wants at the last moment to obtain absolution. He differs from all other Don Juans, including the original one, in becoming, towards the end of his days, a comparatively reformed character. Byron's Don Juan was to have become worse and worse as he grew older, and was at last either to have gone to the infernal regions in the traditional style, or to have contracted an unsuitable marriage; Alfred de

10 *

Musset's Don Juan, under the name of Hassan, is avowedly a poetical expression of the Don Juan imagined by Hoffman (" Hoffmann l'a ou passer au son de la musique "), perpetually in search of an ideal and sacrificing

" Sa beauté, sa gloire, et son génie,
    Pour un être impossible et qui n'existait pas."

The Don Juan, however, of Poushkin is in his last moments if not good at least interesting.   He behaves more insultingly to the statue than any of his predecessors, but in the end becomes transformed through the love with which he inspires and which he himself feels for Donna Anna.   The termination is new and striking, but perhaps not natural; and it may be for that reason that Poushkin, after writing his " Guest of Stone," and keeping it for seven years, had still no thought of publishing it.

CHAPTER XVI.

THE FAUST OF HISTORY AND OF LEGEND.

THE once popular delusion which identified Faust the
magician with Fust or Faust the inventor of the art of
printing from movable types is no longer entertained.
It is just possible, however, that Faust the printer may
have been the father of that Faust, professor of the
black art, around whom have crystallised all the most
remarkable stories that had previously been told of
other magicians from Zoroaster to Simon Magus,
from Theopilus of Syracuse to Robert of Normandy,
and from Pope Sylvester to Cornelius Agrippa, who
lived about the same time as the Faust endeared to us
by poetry, painting, and music, and, like that personage, kept a black dog. There is nothing to show
that Faust the printer had dealings with the devil,

though he seems to have been suspected at one time of corrupt practices.in that direction. The story runs that, after perfecting his system of printing from independent characters, Faust went to Paris, where his invention was not yet known, and there sold as manuscript, and, of course, at a high price, copies of the Latin Bible produced by his new and comparatively inexpensive method. Faust intended to work printing as a secret process, and the sale of printed volumes at the prices usually charged for volumes copied by hand would, no doubt, speedily have enriched him. His customers, however, compared what they had bought; and when it was seen that the words in the pretended manuscripts were, letter by letter, absolutely identical in shape, it was difficult not to conclude that the copies had been mutiplied by unlawful means. Thus John Faust, in the middle of the fifteenth century, by practising an imposition acquired the character of a wizard.

It is quite certain that John Faust the printer, who, unable to patent his invention, had determined to make money out of it by applying it to his own private ends, was not the Faust who, by solemn compact and in return for certain immediate advantages, gave himself over to Satan. Faust the necromancer—calling himself, according to some authorities, George, according to others, John Faust—may, all the same, have been the printer's son. The period of the magician's activity dates from the end of the fifteenth century; and not later than the beginning of the sixteenth we find him installed in the chair of magic at the University of Cracow. "They are not great magicians now," says Heine of contemporary Poles in some remarks on Twardowski, the so-called "Polish Faust," who was doubtless one and the same person as that German Faust who professed sorcery at Cracow. The Poles, however, must have been terribly addicted to magic in the early part of the sixteenth century if, as appears to have been the case, it was thought worth while to maintain at their celebrated university a lecturer on the subject.

One reason for supposing that Professor Faust of Cracow—"Faust, Junior," as he always styled himself —may have belonged to the family of John Faust, the printer of Mayence, is to be found in the lamentable but undeniable fact that he was also given to romancing. Far from denying his alleged connection with the devil, he was in the habit of boasting of his influence in that quarter; and he openly declared that the victories gained by the Emperor's armies in Italy were all due to his occult machinations. The Poles may have been amused by these tales. But Faust's German friends saw no fun in them, and were inclined to look upon their author as the mountebank which he seems really to have been. One of Faust's countrymen, after remarking on the vanity of the man's profession as soothsayer—which, nevertheless, he says, gained for him the admiration of the vulgar—adds: "I heard him chattering in the inn. I did not chastise him for his boasting. What is the madness of another man to me?" Another remarks that "Magister Georgius Sabellicus Faustus, Junior," as the professor of magic called himself, "is a philosopher less remarkable for philosophy than for fatuity, that he ought to be beaten with sticks, and that it is astonishing he can be allowed publicly to confess doctrines and practices condemed by the Church." The priests were naturally very much against him, and accused him of having said that if all the works of Plato and Aristotle were lost, he could rewrite the whole of them with an added grace of his own. He was also charged with having asserted that there was nothing at all wonderful in the miracles of Jesus Christ, all of which he could at any time perform.

The most noteworthy testimony on the subject of this mediæval conjuror and spirit-rapper comes from Melancthon, who was personally acquainted with him. In his "Table Talk," collected by Manlius, Melancthon is represented as saying that he had known "a certain person named Faust," who was professor at Cracow, where he taught magic, who travelled a great deal, had acquired many secrets, and at Venice had astonished the people by flying in the air. The devil, according to Melancthon, raised the magician aloft

but maliciously dropped him, so that he was much injured by the shock, though not killed. His end came
to him in a village in Wurtemburg, where, being very
low-spirited one evening, he in the first place cau-
tioned the innkeeper with whom he lodged not to be
too much terrified if anything alarming happened
during the night. At midnight in fact the house
was shaken by an earthquake ; and the next morning,
Faust not making his appearance, the innkeeper went
into his room and found him lying by the side of his
bed lifeless and with his face turned to the ground—a
sign that he had been killed by the devil. "Until
then," observes the reformer, "he had a dog with him,
which was the devil." Melancthon sums up Faust's
character by calling him "*turpissima bestia et cloaca
multorum diabolorum.*"

Wierus or Weiher, writing in 1588, the year after
that in which the Faust legend appeared in print,
speaks of Faust as a professor of magic at Cracow and
other places, and tells an anecdote of him which is
also to be found in the popular story. Faust, when
from time to time he diverted his mind from the con-
templation of the higher philosophy, was fond of a
practical joke; and meeting one day a man who wished
to be shaved, he proposed, for a sufficient quantum of
wine—to which, according to Wierns, he was addicted
—to perform the operation without soap or razor. The
offer was accepted, when Faust rubbed the man's chin

over with arsenic, and so effectually that not only his beard but his skin also came away.

The compiler and commentator of the second earliest version of the Faust legend, Widman, whose "True History," &c. was printed at Hamburg in 1599, represents Faust, at least in his early days, not as a wine-bibber, but as the sworn enemy of excess both in eating and drinking. Faust had a peculiar horror of drinking before going to bed, and saw death in that "sleeping draught" which Macbeth seems to have taken habitually, and which he expected Lady Macbeth to bring him the last thing at night in whatever business he might happen to be engaged. Faust felt strongly on the subject, and placed his views on record in Latin hexameters and pentameters.

"Credite mortales, noctis potatio mors est,"

is one of his lines, and he wrote a couplet to the same effect in a medical work of which Widman speaks knowingly, as though he himself had seen it. Here is the eminently prosaic couplet :—

"Corporis atque animi mors est impletio ventris ;
Liberat a morbis sobrietas variis."

But from the moment the chroniclers take him in hand, Faust, as we first saw him, " chattering," " boasting," and " astonishing the common people," loses his identity. His actions remain the same, but his character is entirely changed. He keeps a dog, he flies through the air, his house at a critical moment is shaken by an earthquake, and he applies, in facetious moods, his secret shaving-powder to the chins of the vulgar.

Faust's thoughts, however, are now those of his biographer—evidently a theologian of the Reformed Church; and the problems which he sets himself to solve are those which agitated the period in which the materials of what has since been known as the Faust legend were first put together. The so-called story contains more controversy than incidents. Each brief section of narrative is followed by a long section of disquisition; and the result is at once a tale and a tract, in which we are not only informed as to what befell Faust, but are also enlightened as to the errors of the Church of Rome. It is with the evil spirit, the enemy of God and of the human race, that Faust enters into relations; and it is between him and Faust that the real drama takes place. But we are reminded from time to time that on many points, as in regard to celibacy and the reading of the Bible, the views of the evil spirit are identical with those of the Romish clergy. Mephistopheles appears in the garb of a monk —which accounts for the hood, though not for the red cloak (borrowed, apparently, from the Zamiel of *Der Freischütz*), in which he is exhibited on the modern stage; and in telling Faust what subjects he may, and what he must absolutely not discuss, he forbids the Bible, but allows him full liberty to occupy himself with "ceremonies, the mass, purgatory, sophistry, legends, councils, and school theology." Faust prefers higher themes, and, leaving aside the Bible, disputes with Mephistopheles on the relations of the devil towards God, the nature of heaven and hell, the eternity of punishment for sin, and the possibility, in his own particular case, of repentance and reconciliation with the Divine Ruler.

Neither Spiess, the author of the earliest version of the Faust story, published in 1587 (on which Marlowe based his "Dr. Faustus," produced the year afterwards), nor Widman, nor any of the German narrators who have treated this theme, take note of Faust's life in Poland, which, in due time, was made the subject of a second legend, with Polish details, and with Twardowski, a Polonised Faust, substituted for the Faust of Germany.

The Polish Faust behaves with much levity. Like his German cousin, he takes flights in the air in company with his familiar spirit, and, like the Faust of one of the German ballads, he enjoys the right of requiring this spirit to execute three commands—the third of which is that he shall take Madame Twardowska for his wife. Rather than do this, the devil who was already acquainted with the lady broke the compact and Twardowski was saved. This ingenuity on the part of the national magician has been celebrated by the Polish poet Mickievicz in appropriate verse. Is it not remarkable that, whereas the German Faust wished to marry, but was not allowed to do so by Mephistopheles, the Polish Faust, a married man, sought to free himself by diabolical means from his wife? Twardowski seems to have been the only married man who ever sold himself to the devil, though not the only one who endeavoured to escape from his matrimonial responsibilities by getting the devil to relieve him of them. But " Le Mystère du Chevalier qui donna sa Femme au Diable " has very little to do with the Faust legend.

The wife of the wicked knight just spoken of was saved by the intercession of the Holy Virgin. So also was Theophilus of Syracuse when, like Faust, he had signed away his soul. But after the Reformation this means of escape was only within reach of those necromancers who had preserved the Catholic faith. Faust, moreover, was much more advanced in his opinions than the very primitive Theophilus, or than the simple-minded gentleman in the " Contes Dévots," who was willing, if by so doing he could gain the heart of the woman he loved, to forsake God, but would not on any account abandon the Holy Virgin. Faust did not believe in a future state, or at least he had grave doubts on the subject. In his first interviews with Mephistopheles he was uncertain whether he should sell himself at all ; and he felt tolerably confident that if he did sell himself he would be able at the last moment, either through repentance or by some other means, to cheat the devil and regain his liberty. Mephistopheles showed himself willing to make things easy for him, and contented himself, as a first step, with presenting for his consideration, in diplomatic fashion, a little convention in five points.

No. 1 exacted the denial of God; and Faust accepted it without much hesitation, resolved as he was, at a fitting moment, to abjure his impious renunciation. No. 2 obliged him to hate the human race; a condition which grieved him, as his fellow-creatures had done him no harm, and he bore no ill-will towards them. He could not, however, but yield on this point as on the preceding one. No. 3 required him to hate the clergy, who seem to have been regarded by the author of the legend—doubtless himself a clergyman—as holding a midway position between God and man. No. 4 bound him never to set foot in a church; and No. 5 forbade his getting married. As Faust cared neither for Church nor clergy, and he had no wish to get married, he agreed readily to the three last points. Mephistopheles, on his side, pledged himself to execute all Faust's commands during a period of twenty-four years, at the expiration of which term Faust became his, body and soul. When everything was ready, Faust was informed that he must sign with his blood. A vein was opened; the precious liquid was put in a vessel on the fire; it boiled; Mephistopheles handed

Faust a pen, and the business was finished. Meanwhile there had been no question of Helen, still less of Gretchen, of whom no trace or suggestion is to be found in the earliest versions of the Faust legend. The primary object of the baffled magician had been to extend his knowledge; and it was not until later chroniclers had developed the story in various directions that, in connection with Article 5, the shadowy figure of a young German girl was introduced, which took form in subsequent editions, until at last, in the hands of the poet, it bloomed into the personage of Margaret.

CHAPTER XVII.

GRADUAL TRANSFORMATION OF THE FAUST LEGEND.

BUT for the famous fifth point in the treaty between Faust and Mephistopheles, Margaret might never have existed; and now, as in the sixteenth century, the story of Faust would still have remained simply that of his selling himself to the fiend; of his disputations with Mephistopheles on the mysteries of the earth, heaven, and, above all, hell; his repentance; his vain attempts to escape from the power of the devil; his increasing despair as the term of his contract draws to an end; his exhortations to his admirers, the students, that his example may not be lost upon them; and, finally, his death. Helen of Troy, with her " coal-black eyes, cherry lips, and neck like a white swan," as she is described in old Spiess's narrative, would probably not

have been forgotten; though her part in the drama of
Faust's career, despite the fact that she lives with him
as his wife and bears him a son, is not an important
one. Lovers of analogies may, perhaps, say that Helen
is to Faust what Venus—in another legend, based on
the same fundamental idea—is to Tannhäuser. The
principle is laid down in one of the numerous popular
versions of the Faust story that the devil likes "the
word" to be followed by "the deed"; and though
Faust, under pressure, has declared himself in writing
to be the enemy of God, man, the clergy, the Church,
and marriage, he does not, in practice, show himself to
be anything of the kind until Helen is introduced as
if to console him for his inability to take a wife. He
passes time in holding "disputations" with Mephistopheles on high theological and metaphysical subjects;
in playing ridiculous practical jokes; and in summon-
ing to his presence the heroes and other personages
of the Homeric poems—including Polyphemus, whom
the author of the narrative compares with Goliath—
and thereupon launches into the history of Sampson.
At last, in Spiess's original version, Helen appears
and, remaining with Faust, becomes the mother of a
child, who receives the name of Justus. But in the
story of the year 1587 the appearance of Helen does
not follow closely on Faust's unlawful desire to get
married. It was reserved for Widman—who published
his elaborate narrative and commentary twelve years

I.   11

later, and who considered himself better informed than
his predecessor as to the true history of Faust—to
establish the connection between Faust's desire to get
married and the substitution by Mephistopheles of Helen
for the legitimate wife who could not, on any account,
be allowed to him.

In a much shorter version than either of the preceding ones, published in 1728, and described by
Scheible in " Das Kloster " as the first of the " *little*
story-books* " on the subject, Faust's wish to get married takes the form of love for " a beautiful but poor
girl who was in service at a shopkeeper's in his neigh-
bourhood, and who would permit him nothing out of
wedlock." Faust had a very serious quarrel with
Mephistopheles in regard to this damsel; and when
he declared his intention of marrying her, whether
his familiar spirit liked it or not, a mighty wind suddenly arose and shook the house (as when Georgius
Sabellicus Faustus, of the University of Cracow, gave
up the ghost), after which the building burst into
flames, so that Faust was near being tormented with
fire before his time. All the authors testify to the
occurrence of this phenomenon as the emphatic expression of the devil's aversion to matrimony. But
the editor of the narrative published in 1728 seems to
have been the first to show that, as soon as the devil
had frightened Faust out of all idea of marrying the
future Margaret, he at once calmed and demoralised him

by giving him Helen in place of the " beautiful but poor girl who would permit him nothing out of wedlock."

In yet another edition of the Faust legend, dated 1839, and which may possibly therefore have been founded, in part at least, on Goethe's dramatic poem, the Margaret episode, which was destined to be gradually developed until it should at last fill the framework of the whole story, has assumed larger dimensions and gained new features. The " beautiful but poor girl" has become the " beautiful and modest daughter of honourable people," whom Faust, "by the assistance of a procuress, and through rich presents and deceitful promises, befools and brings to ruin." Thereupon, when she became a mother and found herself deserted by her faithless one, " she in distress killed her own infant, and was sentenced to undergo the punishment for child-murder. The story is quite credible," continues the writer. " The devil would take good care that each word given by Faust should be followed by a deed, and when one bears on his soul the soul of another he is already on the way to eternal damnation."

Neither Spiess nor Widman say anything to indicate the existence of a Margaret beyond telling us that Faust wished to get married; from which it may not unreasonably be inferred that there was someone he wished to marry, for we had already been assured that marriage in the abstract possessed no sort of attraction for him. It is remarkable, however, that the charming

11 *

personage who in the end was to become the most
interesting figure in the Faust story, should, in the
earliest versions, have had no definite existence. Her
place in the tale was already marked from the
beginning. She is the natural dramatic consequence of
Article 5, which Faust was bound to observe, and
which he is led, through the unconscious girl, to set at
defiance, that he may fall more surely into the power
of the fiend. But though century by century she
grew in importance, it was not until Goethe breathed
into her the breath of poetic life that this innocent and
suffering agent in the damnation of Faust was known
by a name. Since Goethe's time, Margaret, adopted
by painters, dramatists, and composers, has had new
beauty bestowed upon her, or, at least, has had her
own native beauty presented in new lights. Rembrandt
painted Faust, Christopher Van Sichem painted Faust
and Mephistopheles. But Ary Scheffer painted Margaret and scenes in which Margaret is always the
principal figure. In Goethe's *Faust* the first part—
what is generally accepted as the whole work—ends
with the death of Margaret; nor does the real drama
commence until Margaret is accosted by Faust as she
leaves the cathedral, in which we afterwards see her
unable to utter a prayer. Margaret, moreover, as a
lyrical personage in the fullest sense of the word, could
not but engage the attention of composers; of whom the
first to set her beautiful songs to music was Schubert.

When, fifty years ago, Prince Puckler-Muskau told
Goethe that he had seen *Faust* performed with
music by Prince Radziwill, the venerable poet replied
that " it must have been very strange." Far stranger
would the ingeniously constructed—or rather, cleverly
trimmed—drama of *Faust and Margaret* have appeared
to him; and curious indeed would he have found the
opera composed by M. Gounod on the *Faust and Margaret* drama as converted by its skilful arrangers,
MM. Barbier and Carré, into a libretto. Herr Wagner
has expressed in " Opera and Drama," needless indignation at the thought of *William Tell* having been set to
music by an Italian ; and he has at least equally good
reasons for complaining that *Faust* should have had
what threatens to be its permanent operatic form given
to it by a Frenchman. The French have, indeed, during
the last thirty or forty years, shown a peculiar persis-
tency in taking as a subject for music what they knew
perfectly well to be a German legend. Three French
composers of different degrees and kinds of talent,
Mdlle. Louise Bertin, Hector Berlioz, and M. Gounod,
have sinned in this manner ; and to speak only of
M. Gounod's charming opera, it must be admitted that
the two principal male personages of that work, wandering about as if in search of adventures, bear a far
greater resemblance to the Lionel and Plunkett of
Flotow's *Martha,* than to the Faust and Mephistopheles
of necromantic tradition. Goethe's *Faust* was never

intended for the stage; nor even in the abridged stage version prepared for the German theatres could it ever have become a popular stage-play. M. Gounod's opera, on the other hand, has pleased the public everywhere, and nowhere more than in Germany, where, however, the managers, to mark their sense of the difference that exists between the work of the German poet and that of the French dramatist and composer, give to the latter the name, not of *Faust*, but of *Margaret*.

Thus in the course of three centuries the popular story of " Faust " has gradually become transformed into the opera of " Margaret." It is for Margaret, according to Gounod's opera, that Faust sells himself; and Margaret having been loved, ruined, and abandoned, Mephistopheles claims Faust as his prey. The Faust story is converted into the story of an aged student who gives himself to the devil for renewed youth and the love of a pretty girl, and who is carried off to the devil as soon as the pretty girl has been destroyed, in body and mind, if not in soul. The public might say to Margaret, in the eloquent words of Faust himself,—

> " One look, one word, from you is more to me
> Than all the teachings of philosophy."

They prefer the story of Margaret's love to the record of Faust's disputations with Mephistopheles, and the history of his spiritual experience as he finds himself sinking more and more hopelessly into the power of the devil. Neither in Goethe's *Faust*, nor in the Faust of the story-books, is the principal personage carried off to the infernal regions for his conduct to Margaret, which, if it could make angels weep, from devils could only elicit a smile. In Germany, as in England, the idea has got abroad that at the end of the First Part Faust is seized and borne away. So indeed he is, but to fresh adventures, not to eternal torments. Otherwise the action in the second part would take place in the lower world; and " Helen of Troy" would not be Helen resuscitated, but Helen's ghost. Goethe seems to have intended at one time to follow in the second part, as he had done in the first, the main incidents of the popular story. After the "beautiful but poor girl" of whom Faust became enamoured, but whom he was not allowed to marry, comes, as an essential part of the tale, the brilliant Helen with whom there would be no question of marriage. In the old legend Faust further visits the Court of the Emperor, and this also he does in Goethe's second part.

The last three years of Faust's life in the old story-books—as also in Marlowe's *Doctor Faustus,* based on Spiess's narrative—are passed night after night in mental and moral torments, of which in the operatic version of Goethe's dramatic poem we naturally find no more trace than in the poem itself. The Faust of Spiess and of Widman's narrative repents and is thereupon called to account by Mephistopheles and forced to renew his engagement, so that there can be no mistake about the matter. He then questions his " dear Mephistopheles " more earnestly than ever as to the nature of eternal punishment; and Mephistopheles civilly explains it to him by the image of a stone, which heated, made red-hot, and left to cool, may be heated again and again for an indefinite period. " The pain of hell consists," moreover says Mephistopheles, " in hell's lying at the foot of heaven, from which the infernal abyss is plainly visible but quite inaccessible." Vividly realising the terrors of his approaching end, Faust now suffers so much that one night he wakes Mephistopheles and asks him if he is not already in hell. Mephistopheles scouts the idea. " The torments that await the damned go far beyond all that can be pictured by the imagination," he tells him, adding, when Faust shudders with alarm, that he is grieved to see him so timid. " Put a bold face on the matter," he continues, with truly diabolical pleasantry, " and think of the number of Jews, Saracens, and sinners of all kinds whom you will have with you." Before his death, Faust, who had already written his memoirs for the benefit of humanity, addresses some few last words to the students. He prays in vain that the devil, while torturing his body to all eternity, will yet spare his soul. Then at night a noise of hissing and shrieking is heard; and when the students enter the room the next morning they find the remains of the unhappy doctor scattered about the floor.

Of Zito, the Bohemian Faust, some account may be found in Scheible's "Kloster." Zito possesses neither the intellectual elevation nor the spiritual aspirations of the Faust celebrated by Spiess and Widman. But he mystifies peasants, cheats horse-dealers, and indulges in various shaves, including the removal of the beard by means of arsenic, like the Faustus of the German chroniclers and of our own Marlowe.

Twardowski, the Polish Faust, besides being a great practical joker, is popularly believed—as was at one time the Faust of Germany—to have invented printing. His life may be studied in a monograph with illustrations published some seventeen years ago at Vienna, under the title of "Twardowski; oder Der Polnischer Faust." Entering Russia from Poland in the year 1863, with a copy of this harmless work in my possession, I was required to give it up; and on claiming it afterwards at the Censor's office at Moscow, where it had been sent on, was assured that it was a political pamphlet of a most revolutionary character. "Twardowski," said the far-seeing officials, " represents Poland, the devil is Russia, and the author of this insidious publication would show that Poland is bound to Russia by a contract of diabolical origin." Thus, several centuries after his death, Twardowski was still destined to mystify the vulgar. I, however, was the victim of his last practical joke, for my life of Twardowski was confiscated.

CHAPTER XVIII.

HOW DR. FAUST BECAME A DANCER.

As if with a presentiment that never would another man have dealings with the devil, the old story-tellers repeated of Faust all the tales that had ever been told of anyone else in the same position. Thus Faust took miraculous flights like Robert the Devil, like Pope Sylvester, and like Simon Magus, who is reported to have raised himself in the air before Nero and to have been brought down suddenly to the ground by a counter miracle performed by the apostles Peter and Paul. Indeed, in connection with Faust's atmospheric expeditions, the writer of the oldest version of the Faust story points out that our Saviour was similarly carried by Satan to the roof of the temple and to the summit of the mount. Like Cornelius Agrippa and the aforesaid Pope Sylvester, Faust kept a dog whose eyes on

occasion glared till they looked like coals of fire. Like
Zito, the Bohemian magician, he in one of his gay
moments transformed a horse and cart into a bundle of
hay. Like Sylvester, and like Twardowski, the Pole, he
suffered from that " damned equivocation of the fiend,"
which also troubled a certain Scottish gentleman who
had transactions with the infernal powers; for as the
"fiend," after making his victim swear never to go to
Jerusalem or to Rome, contrived to catch Sylvester
in the Jerusalem church at a place called Rome,
near Cracow, so by a similar trick Mephistopheles
caught Faust.   Sylvester, surprised by the devil's
agent preaching inside " Jerusalem," when he had
sworn never to go to Jerusalem ("a place forbidden
to us devils," he had been told), was held to be
checkmated; and he was carried off to the infernal
regions, his dog, which he had left outside the
church, howling dismally the while.   Twardowski,
being still entitled to demand the execution of one
remaining wish, called upon the devil to marry his wife,
Madame Twardowski; a requisition which so alarmed
the evil spirit that, breaking his compact, he took to
flight, leaving Twardowski a free man. In some versions of the Faust legend, Faust is similarly entrapped
at an inn, of which Rome is the sign; while in yet
another version he entraps Mephistopheles by proposing
to him the alternative of going to Rome or breaking
his compact, and would have discomfited him altogether

had not Mephistopheles suddenly, by way of last card, produced Helen of Troy, through whose charms Faust is once more brought within the devil's power. Neither, however, in Spiess's or in Widman's ancient narrative, does this incident occur, but only in a popular ballad on the Faust subject, much later in origin than the Spiess and Widman books.

Besides the rhymed ballads and the popular narratives great and small—that of Widman is a prose epic with a commentary appended to each book—the Faust subject was treated in puppet-show dramas and popular plays, and the dramatic history of Faust began, as everyone knows, in England. Heine, in his " Doktor Faust, ein Tanz-Poem "—being the libretto of a ballet which he wrote in 1850 for Mr. Lumley, but which was never produced—derives the subject of Marlowe's *Faust* partly from the impressive old story published by Spiess, partly from an Anglo-Saxon version of the legend of Theophilus which Heine supposes Rutebœuf, the *trouvère*, to have borrowed for his Miracle of Theophilus.

But though Theophilus of Syracuse is usually regarded as Faust's direct ancestor, there are remarkable points of difference between the legend in which Theophilus figures and that in which Faust plays the principal part. Theophilus (as to whose doings Sir George Dasent, in English, and M. Achille Jubinal, in French, may be profitably consulted) was an ecclesiastic who, having modestly and in good faith declared himself "unwilling to become a bishop," was by the bishop who replaced him deposed from his office as Vidame (Vice-dominus) ; and, thereupon, finding himself ruined and disgraced, sold himself, through a Hebrew magician, to the devil, but ultimately got saved through the intercession of the Holy Virgin, who herself went to hell in order to get back the compact. In the original story, written in Greek, by Eutychianus, a pupil of Theophilus, the narrator declares that he himself saw the devil engaged in conversation with Theophilus, and that he witnessed (not, however, in a legal sense) the signing of the deed, which was of course done in the blood of the victim.

The main features of this legend of the sixth century were reproduced some centuries later by an anonymous bard in Latin hexameters, beginning "Miles clarus erat" ; the most important variation being the substitution in the Latin poem of a soldier for the priest of the original Greek narrative in prose. But the story was destined to be made popular by Rutebœuf, whose *Miracle de Théophile* found its way from the north of France both to England and to Germany. The old English or "Anglo-Saxon" version of the legend of Theophilus—as Heine, writing in the days before Freeman, ventured to call it—may, of course, have been known to Marlowe. But a German writer has distinctly shown, in a work on the "Earliest Dramatic Treatment of the Faust subject," that Marlowe based his work on the story of Dr. Faustus, as given in the narrative published by Spiess. It is difficult to see what he could have borrowed from the legend of Theophilus, who sells himself, not like Faust, to extend his knowledge beyond human limits, but from pique, from poverty, and for the sake of material enjoyment. Theophilus, moreover, is saved through the intercession of the Holy Virgin ; whereas Faust, who is a Protestant, has no such resource open to him, and is left in the spirit of tragedy and of human life to meet the fate he has himself invited.

The signing of the compact in blood drawn from the victim's own veins is an incident which occurs both in the legend of Theophilus and in the old Faust story. But it is only in the Faust story that the blood, trickling down the man's hand, forms in the palm the letters H. F., which are interpreted as meaning " Homo fuge " ; and it is to be observed that this detail is reproduced by Marlowe, who has, indeed, followed the old narrative very closely, and is indebted to it, not only for incidents, but also for some of the finest thoughts in his admirable work.

Heine, when he discussed the subject of Faust in " Die romantische Schule," was convinced that the historical Faust was the old printer of that name ; the " same Faust," in his own words, "who invented printing, and who lived at a time when people were beginning to preach against the powerful authority of the

Church, and independently to attack it." Apart from the dislike which the Church, if it could have foreseen to what results the invention would lead, might well have entertained for printing, the monastic orders have been accused of objecting to it as putting an end to the copying trade, of which they had practically a monopoly.

Thus the story that Faust the printer was sold to the devil might have had its origin simply in the malice of the clergy, whose interests were threatened by his invention. A serious joker, however, has argued that Faust the printer was called "professor of the black art," because the art in which he worked was literally a black one. If Faust the printer had ever been suspected by his contemporaries, or by the generation immediately succeeding his own, of having sold himself to the devil, the most rational explanation of the notion would be the astonishment of the public at the power he possessed, and which he exercised in secret, of multiplying copies of a book rapidly and without limit as to number. But neither the contemporaries of John Faust the printer, who died towards 1470, nor those of George Faust—"Faust, Junior," as he called himself —who was in full activity as professor of magic at Cracow in the first years of the sixteenth century, seem to have known anything of the rumour set going at a later period as to the printer's relations with the infernal powers.

When, nearly twenty years after the publication of "Die Romantische Schule," Heine undertook to compose a ballet on the subject of Faust, he put aside the old printer, and recognised the fact that the Faust of necromantic tradition was the professor of Cracow, spoken of by Luther, Melancthon, Weiher, and the Abbot Tritheim of Wurzburgh, and with whom Melancthon, according to Manlius, the collector of his "Table Talk," was well acquainted. Heine, like Meyerbeer in similar circumstances, knew better than to touch the *Faust* of Goethe. M. Blaze de Bury has told us, in his recollections of Meyerbeer, that that great composer could not be induced to undertake an opera on the subject of Faust, which, he held, had already received its appropriate and permanent form. He was willing to set the songs to music and to furnish interludes, but would not hear of the work itself being reduced to the shape and style of a libretto. If Meyerbeer shrunk from the idea of making Gretchen a prima donna, still less could Heine think of turning her into a *première danseuse*. There is no question, then, of Margaret in Heine's "Tanz-Poem."

But if Margaret belongs to Goethe, Dr. Faust belongs to everyone. He had been dealt with at least fifty authors, of whom two—Marlowe and the anonymous writer of the old story-books published by Spiess—were true poets, before Goethe took him in hand. There are a dozen printed versions extant of the Faust story, in prose and in verse, and as many of the puppet-show plays and other popular dramas on the same subject, which, with performers who improvised the details, assumed new features according as they were represented at Ulm, at Strasburg, at Augsburg, at Cologne, or at Berlin; while, apart from Goethe's work, about thirty pieces based on the Faust legend had been produced at regular theatres in Germany up to the time (1829) when the *Faust* of Goethe was first put on the stage.

Faust had even been made into a ballet more than a century before Heine agreed so to treat it for Her Majesty's Theatre. A playbill of the Vienna Opera House, which Scheible (who reproduces it in *Das Kloster*) assigns to the year 1730, announces the performance of a ballet called *Dr. Faust*, which is to combine the features of "German comedy, English pantomime, and Italian opera." A programme of the action of the piece sets forth that in the opening scene Faust, wearied with vain study, is tempted by Mephistopheles who offers to place before him "the most beautiful women from all the four quarters of the globe." After a little hesitation, Faust consents to sign the usual compact, and the scene terminates, like the first act of Gounod's opera, with a duet for Faust and Mephistopheles.

In Heine's ballet, to which, as Mr. Lumley has told us in his "Memoirs," the name of *Mephistophela* was

12

to have been given (it was, indeed, published under that title in the " Revue des Deux Mondes," though Heine, in the German version published at Hamburg in 1851, calls it *Der Doktor Faust*) a whole series of beautiful women are exhibited by the female Mephistopheles for the entertainment of her victim. But instead of being women of no individuality from various parts of the world, as in the old Viennese ballet, the apparitions with which Heine's choregraphic Faust is gratified are dancing celebrities of the highest character. As history and the Bible do not yield a sufficient number of eminent female dancers to supply the requirements of a ballet designed on the model of Heine's *Mephistophela*, the author introduced a certain number of male dancers; which presupposes on the part of Dr. Faust a passion, not merely for dancing girls with beautiful figures, graceful movements, and expressive gestures, but a passion for dancing as an art. Thus Mephistophela is made to call up and exhibit to Faust " David dancing before the ark " ; a scene which, if presented at Her Majesty's Theatre, would scarcely have been applauded, would, perhaps, have been hissed, and might even have been hooted.

Heine, in publishing his *Doktor Faust*, gave with it an introduction and a commentary ; and it can scarcely be disrespectful to this wittiest of poets and most poetical of wits to say in regard to the " Tanz-Poem " that the introduction and commentary are the best part of it. No English reader need be told why Heine's *Mephistophela* was never produced in England. The amiable Mr. Lumley assured Heine that the ballet-master objected to the work for technical reasons; and Heine thereupon wrote, in the introduction to *Der Doktor Faust*, that, as there had been no previous instance of a poet's composing a piece for dancers, *Mephistophela* had been refused "*par esprit de corps de ballet*." He forgot that his friend, Théophile Gautier, had, on the basis of Heine's own beautiful legend, composed the ballet of *Giselle*, in which Perrot, Mr. Lumley's ballet-master, who was alleged to have refused *Mephistophela*, had so often appeared with his beautiful wife, Carlotta Grisi.

A female Mephistopheles is intelligible enough. But though, from the witch of Endor to the witches who appeared to Macbeth, and from the Amber witch to the witches who, not two centuries ago, were drowned at Paisley, there have always been women who were reputed to have dealings with the devil, yet we should look in vain for a female counterpart to Faust.

CHAPTER XIX.

THE OPERATIC FAUST.

NEVER was a more generally successful opera produced than the beautiful work in music constructed by M. Gounod on the literary framework manufactured for him by Messrs. Barbier and Carré out of Goethe's *Faust*. " Ary Scheffer's Gretchen," said Heine, "is indeed Goethe's Gretchen, but she has read all Schiller"; and when Scheffer's own graceful representation of Goethe's Gretchen, penetrated with the spirit of Schiller, is set to music by Gounod, the result is the operatic Marguerite—or, by a final transformation, " Margherita "—whom we all know, but whom Goethe would perhaps not have recognised. The old poet could scarcely, however, have declined to accept this charming personage as his own offspring, or at least as

his own descendant. " *Cela doit être de moi,*" said M.
Thiers, when he was asked whether he was the author
of an admirable discourse on the death of Marshal
Gouvion de St. Cyr, which Armand Carrel had written,
and of which Mr. Disraeli had just delivered a spirited
" adaptation " in the House of Commons on the occasion of the death of the Duke of Wellington; and
Goethe, had the operatic Margherita pleased him, and
had he not cared to disavow her grandfather the Dutch
painter, and her father the French composer, would
have had the fullest right to claim the beautiful child
in the character of great-grandfather. The original
Gretchen was a much more homely flower than the
species of white lily presented to us by Patti, Nilsson,
and Albani, whose refined impersonation reminds one
of the Princess Elsa, daughter of King Henry the
Fowler, rather than of the little maid whose hands were
so coarse from house-work that she wondered how
Faust could kiss them, and who was so ignorant (she
had certainly not read Schiller) that she could not
understand how so accomplished a gentleman could
take any interest in her conversation. Goethe's
Gretchen tells the simple truth when she says that she
is "not a lady." But this legendary utterance, proceed-
ing from the lady-like, and at the same time saint-like,
young girl that Gretchen becomes when Scheffer has
given her visible grace and Gounod has taught her to
sing, savours a little of affectation and in some mea-

sure justifies the coquettish view which Mdme. Lucca
takes of the character—especially in the first interview
of Margherita with Faust.

Besides being very charming, the part of Margherita
is also very fatiguing. In the first act she is, like the
good child in the nursery precept, "seen but not
heard." In the second act she sings but one phrase—
the retort uncourteous to Faust complimenting her
and offering her his arm. In the third act she scarcely
leaves the stage; and she has to sing the ballad of
the King of Thule, the jewel song, and some hundred
bars of the most beautiful music ever written in the
never-ending duet. In the fourth act she is again
almost constantly in presence of the audience; and in
the scene of Valentine's death, and again in the
cathedral scene, is always in very dramatic, very effective, but also very trying situations. In the prison
scene of the fifth act she is once more the central
dramatic figure, and has once more to make her
voice heard almost continuously; to make it heard,
too, above other voices, and, what is more important,
above an orchestra which in the crescendo of the trio
rages like a storm.

Our Margheritas may be generally divided into fair-
haired and dark-haired Margheritas; Margheritas who,
being of a serious cast of mind, take a sentimental
view of the character, and Margheritas who, being
vivacious, regard it in a lively aspect. The original

Margherita, Mdme. Miolan-Carvalho, used to go through
the part in fixed attitudes, imitated from Ary Scheffer,
and with a dreamy trance-like expression of countenance which, at the Théâtre Lyrique, was considered
peculiarly German; though Mdme. Lucca, the favourite
representative of M. Gounod's heroine at Berlin, has
never considered it necessary to adopt this non-natural
and early-Christian manner.

The story of " Faust and Margaret " would not be
very interesting—indeed it would be slightly common-
place—but for the introduction of the supernatural
element. The tenors, however, who impersonate Faust
are not, as a rule, sufficiently mindful of this. They
go through the part with the ordinary love-making
gestures of the Italian operatic stage, and, in fact,
reduce it to the level of the " walking gentleman " of
English comedy, or, at best, the *"premier amoureux"*
of French drama.

In the first account ever published of Mephistopheles,
Faust himself describes his diabolical attendant as " the
emissary now present, Mephistopheles by name, servant
of the Prince Infernal in the East," to whom he assigns
his soul for value to be received. In a formal compact nothing, of course, is said about the garb of the
persons signing it. But the narrator of the original
story makes Mephistopheles appear in the hood and
cloak of a monk. Goethe introduces him in the
apparel of a travelling scholar; and in the second act

of Goethe's dramatic poem Mephistopheles speaks of
himself as wearing a red jacket laced with gold, and a
cap with a cock's feather in it : not a scarlet tunic with
continuations to match—the costume now in favour with
our leading baritones. He advises Faust to dress precisely
like him ; and, while it is probable that the two intimate
friends would have adopted similar fashions, it is certain
that Faust could not have shown himself in public with
a servant of the " Prince Infernal of the East " clothed
in the flaming livery of his master.   Margaret, with
her spiritual vision, sees clearly enough that Mephistopheles is a demon; but Martha, viewing him with the
eye of the body, finds him a perfect gentleman both in
appearance and manners.   The Zamiel of *Der Frei-*
schütz, who appears only at rare intervals in a wood to
an accompaniment of thunder and lightning, may
wear fire-coloured garments and compromise no one.
Mephistopheles, however, has assumed the part of a man
of the world, and to act it with success must first of all
look it. Despite the miraculous character of many of the
incidents, there is no reason why such portions of the
Faust drama as allow of it should not be played with
some regard to nature; and it is not natural that Faust
should associate habitually and constantly with a devil
in scarlet, and that the said devil should be accepted by
students and townspeople as, more or less, one of themselves.   Mephistopheles is in the first act a travelling
scholar, in the second a gentleman, as they say in the

police reports, " of fashionable exterior "; and this last character he maintains until Margaret is tormented by him in the cathedral scene, where his language, however natural from a member of the diabolical service, is quite unworthy of the part he has assumed on earth. " *Sei dannata!* " " *Dannata sei!* " he keeps repeating—words which literally translated into English would be singularly offensive. Here Mephistopheles shows himself the fiend he really is, and might be presented with hoofs and a tail. But in the first three acts, and until the middle of the fourth, he has, together with a very sinister expression of countenance, " the scholar's, courtier's, soldier's eye, tongue, sword."

It need scarcely be pointed out that neither the old men's chorus nor the chorus of soldiers in the fourth act belongs essentially to the drama of *Faust*, and that neither of them has much to do with the high esteem in which the opera is held by musicians. The old men's chorus, as parent of a whole family of similar choruses given by the composers of opéras-bouffes to one-armed soldiers, wooden-legged sailors, and other invalids, deserves to be solemnly cursed at a universal council of musicians, under the presidency, say, of Herr Wagner, who would willingly add to the general condemnation the force of his own personal anathema. The tune given to the old citizens is quaint enough, and it would be difficult, perhaps, to prove, *a priori*, that the chorus is an error in art. But if there had

not been something radically wrong in such a conception, it would scarcely have commended itself to the
attention of MM. Offenbach, Lecocq, Hervé, and the
minor masters of opéra-bouffe. If each character in
an opera ought to have the voice of his age, the father
of William Tell would be unable to sing a *sostenuto*
passage; and Jemmy, his curiously-named son—a
youth of thirteen or fourteen—would have the cracked
voice of adolescence, which would have a much more
original effect than the cracked voice of senility.

Is it necessary to enter once more upon the discussion
whether Mdlle. Pauline Lucca's " reading " of the part
of Margaret is the true reading, and ought she to be
reproved for being coquettish, and for giving the too-
forward Faust from the very beginning that encourage-
ment which, for a little while at least, she should have
seemed to withhold? As for the public, it is delighted
with Mdlle. Lucca's Margaret as Mdlle. Lucca has conceived the character, or at least as she represents it—
for it is not at all certain that our prime donne form
beforehand any distinct conception of the characters
they are about to impersonate. If any amateur of
inquiring mind wishes to know how and why Mdlle.
Lucca's Margherita differs from Mdlle. Nilsson's Margherita, do not let him waste time in studying the
character of Goethe's Gretchen; let him rather study
the temperament and individual peculiarities of the
two prime donne. ┆ The character of Gretchen is little

more than a glass shade which covers and displays now
the talent and beauty of Mdlle. Nilsson, now the
beauty and talent of Mdlle. Lucca. The music does the
rest; and Mdlle. Lucca—for it is of her Margherita in
particular that we are now speaking—being a vocalist
of true sentiment as well as of great executive ability, is
tender in the love-passages, brilliant in the jewel song,
pathetic in the scene of the cathedral, and tragic in the
scene of the prison. Liking and admiring Mdlle.
Lucca, we like to admire Mdlle. Lucca's Margherita.
It may not be Margherita according to Gounod; but it
is at least Margherita according to Mdlle. Lucca, and
that is enough. And seriously, when operatised, the
Gretchen of Goethe ought to lose something of the
roughness and abruptness by which her character in
the drama is marked. "I am neither a young lady,
nor am I pretty, and I don't want your escort," is her
first speech to Faust; and afterwards, when Faust
kisses her hand, she says to him, "Do not kiss it, it
is so rough," and explains that it is her lot to do a
considerable amount of housework. She used to be
very fond of her little sister; but she congratulates
herself on having more leisure now that her little
sister is dead. All this is as unlike Mdlle. Lucca as
possible. Mdlle. Lucca is both lady-like and pretty,
and she knows it, and, in Margherita's position, would
at least not have refused Faust's escort with any unnecessary harshness. Her hands are certainly not

rough, and she cannot be suspected of doing duty as maid-of-all-work. She is not the heroine of common life, who remains the heroine of common life until she is raised above all common things and transfigured by love. She softens without heightening, and refines without spiritualising, the character from the very outset; and considering how many important, almost fundamental, changes have been introduced into the drama of *Faust* in the process of converting it into an opera, one may well say that the least objectionable of all is the alteration which the character of Margaret is made to undergo.

189

CHAPTER XX.

THE FLYING DUTCHMAN.

THE story of the Flying Dutchman can, according to
Dr. Hueffer, be traced back as far as the sixteenth century, and, like that of his fellow-sufferer by land, the
Wandering Jew, "seems to be an outgrowth of the
thoroughly revolutionised and exalted state of feeling
caused by the two great events of those times—the
discovery of a new world by the Spaniards, and of a
new faith by the Germans." Captain Vanderdecken
tries to double the Cape of Good Hope in a heavy
gale; and finding this task too much for him, swears
(to borrow what Dr. Hueffer has written on this
subject in his interesting and valuable work, "The
Music of the Future") "that he will carry out his
purpose even if he should have to sail till Doomsday.
The evil one, hearing this oath, accepts it in its most

literal meaning, and in consequence the unfortunate
sailor is doomed to roam for ever and aye on the
ocean, far from his wife and his beloved Holland.
However, the poets of later ages, pitying the weary
wanderer of the main, have tried in different ways to
release him from this desolate fate. Captain Marryat,
in his well-known novel, has not been very fortunate
in this respect. Another *dénouement* of the story was
invented by Heinrich Heine, and upon this Wagner has
avowedly based the poem of his opera. In Heine's
fragmentary story, ' The Memoirs of Herr von Schna-
belewopski,' the hero (who, by-the-bye, shows only
slightly disguised the characteristic features of the
great humorist himself) tells us how, on his passage
from Hamburg to Amsterdam, he saw a vessel with
blood-red sails, very likely the phantom ship of the
Flying Dutchman, whom shortly afterwards he beheld,
in ipsissimá personá, on the stage of the last-named
city.

"The new feature added to the old story is this, that
instead of an unconditional sentence, Vanderdecken is
condemned to wander till Doomsday, unless he shall
have been released by the love of a woman ' faithful
unto death.' The devil (stupid as he is) does not believe in the virtue of women, and therefore allows the
unhappy captain to go ashore once every seven years
in order to take a wife. The poor Dutchman has been
disappointed in his attempts at finding such a paragon

of faithful spouses for many a time, till at last, just after another period of seven years has elapsed, he meets a Scotch (according to Wagner, a Norwegian) merchant, and readily obtains his paternal consent to a proposed marriage with his daughter. This daughter herself has formed a romantic attachment for the unfortunate sailor, whose story she has heard, and whose picture hangs in her room. When she sees the real Flying Dutchman, she recognises him at once by the resemblance with his likeness, and heroically deciding to share his fate, accepts the offer of his hand. At this moment Schnabelewopski-Heine is (by an unforeseen and indescribable incident) called away from the house, and when he comes back is just in time to see the Dutchman on board his own ship, which is weighing anchor for another voyage of hopeless despair. He loves his bride, and would save her from the fate that threatens her if she accompanies him. But she, 'faithful unto death,' ascends a high rock, and throws herself into the waves, by which heroic deed the spell is broken, and the Flying Dutchman, united with his bride, enters the long-closed gates of eternal rest.

" Heine pretends, as we have said, to have seen this acted on the Amsterdam stage; this statement, however, he withdrew afterwards, and emphatically claimed as his own the invention of the beautiful and eminently dramatic episode. The former statement was also in so far inaccurate that he never sailed from Hamburg to Holland; his voyage was, on the contrary, directed to London, and here most likely it was also that he made the acquaintance of the Flying Dutchman in a theatrical capacity. The story of the Phantom Ship seems to have been at that time (1827), to a certain extent, popular in England. A very impressive version of it had appeared in 'Blackwood's Magazine' (May 1821), and this was made the groundwork of a melo-dramatic production of the late Mr. Fitzball, a play-wright of those days, whose adaptations were as numerous and quite as 'original' as those of some contemporary stage favourites.

"The piece in question is extremely silly, and bad in every respect. Mynheer Vanderdecken here is the slave and ally of some horrid monster of the deep, and his motive in taking a wife is only to increase the number of his victims. In this wicked purpose, how-ever, he does not succeed, the heroine escaping his snares and marrying (if I remember rightly) a young officer whom she had loved against the will of her father. This piece was running at the Adelphi Theatre about the time of Heine's visit to London; and no-thing is more probable than that the German poet, who conscientiously studied the English stage, should have seen it. For the circumstance of the Dutchman's taking a wife, Heine would in that case be indebted to Fitzball, in whose piece there also occurs an old picture connected with the story. It would thus be most interesting to note how Heine developed out of these trivial indications his noble idea of the Dutchman's deliverance by the love of a woman. Wagner, on his part, has heightened the dramatic pathos of the fable by making his hero symbolise a profound philosophical idea—thus raising the conception of his character from the sphere of a popular tale into that of artistic significance, out of fancy into imagination. The pitiful figure of Mynheer Vanderdecken becomes an embodiment of life-weariness longing for death and forgetfulness of individual pain and struggle or (which is the same) of existence."

The impressive version of the "Flying Dutchman" referred to by Dr. Hueffer was told by the writer in "Blackwood," under the not very significant title of "Vanderdecken's Message Home, or the Tenacity of Natural Affection." The story as presented by Wagner, after Heine, has a much deeper meaning; and now that the tale has undergone what may probably be regarded as its final transformation, it may be interesting to see in what shape it was originally presented.

" Our ship," says the writer in " Blackwood," " after touching at the Cape, went out again, and soon losing sight of the Table Mountain, began to be assailed by the impetuous attacks of the sea, which is well known to be more formidable there than in most parts of the known ocean. The day had grown dull and hazy, and the breeze, which had formerly blown fresh, now sometimes subsided almost entirely, and then recovering its strength for a short time, and changing its direction, blew with temporary violence, and died away again, as if exercising a melancholy caprice. A heavy swell began to come from the south-east. Our sails flapped against the masts, and the ship rolled from side to side, as heavily as if she had been water-logged. There was so little wind that she would not steer.

"At 2 P.M. we had a squall, accompanied by thunder and rain. The seamen, growing restless, looked anxiously ahead. They said we would have a dirty night of it, and that it would not be worth while to turn into their hammocks. As the second mate was describing a gale he had encountered off Cape Race, Newfoundland, we were suddenly taken all aback, and the blast came upon us furiously. We continued to scud under a double-reefed mainsail and foretopsail till dusk; but, as the sea ran high, the captain thought it safest to bring her to. The watch on deck consisted of four men, one of whom was appointed to keep a lookout ahead, for the weather was so hazy that we could not see two cables' length from the bows. This man, whose name was Tom Willis, went frequently to the bows, as if to observe something; and when the others called to him, inquiring what he was looking at, he would give no definite answer. They therefore went also to the bows, and appeared startled, and at first said nothing; but presently one of them cried, ' William, go call the watch.'

" The seamen, having been asleep in their hammocks, murmured at this unreasonable summons, and called to know how it looked upon deck. To which Tom Willis replied, ' Come up and see. What we are minding is not on deck, but ahead.'

" On hearing this, they ran up without putting on their jackets; and when they came to the bows, there was a whispering.

" One of them asked, ' Where is she? I do not see her.' To which another replied, ' The last flash of lightning showed there was not a reef in one of her sails; but we, who know her history, know that all her canvas will never carry her into port.'

" By this time the talking of the seamen had brought some of the passengers on deck. They could see nothing, however, for the ship was surrounded by thick darkness and by the noise of the dashing waters, and the seamen evaded the questions that were put to them.

" At this juncture the chaplain came on deck. He was a man of grave and modest demeanour, and was much liked among the seamen, who called him Gentle George. He overheard one of the men asking another, ' if he had ever seen the " Flying Dutchman" before, and if he knew the story about her?' To which the other replied, 'I have heard of her beating about these seas. What is the reason she never reaches port?'

"The first speaker replied, 'They give different reasons for it, but my story is this: She was an Amsterdam vessel, and sailed from that port seventy years ago. Her master's name was Vanderdecken. He was a staunch seaman, and would have his own way, in spite of the devil. For all that, never a sailor under him had reason to complain; though how it is on board with them now, nobody knows. The story is this; that in doubling the Cape, they were a long day trying to weather the Table Bay, which we saw this morning. However, the wind headed them, and went against them more and more, and Vanderdecken walked the deck swearing at the wind. Just after sunset a vessel spoke him, asking if he did not mean to go into the bay that night. Vanderdecken replied, "May I be eternally d—d if I do, though I should beat about here till the day of judgment!" And to be sure, Vander-decken never did go into that bay; for it is believed that he continues to beat about in these seas still, and will do so long enough. This vessel is never seen but with foul weather along with her.'

"To which another replied, 'We must keep clear of her. They say that her captain mans his jolly boat, when a vessel comes in sight, and tries hard to get alongside to put letters on board, but no good comes to them who have communication with him.'

"Tom Willis said, 'There is such a sea between us at present as should keep us safe from such visits.'

"To which the other answered, 'We cannot trust to that if Vanderdecken sends out his men.'

"Some of this conversation having been overheard by the passengers, there was a commotion among them. In the meantime, the noise of the waves against the vessel could scarcely be distinguished from the sounds of the distant thunder. The wind had extinguished the light in the binnacle, where the compass was, and no one could tell which way the ship's head lay. The passengers were afraid to ask questions, lest they should augment the secret sensation of fear which chilled every heart, or learn any more than they already knew. For while they attributed their agitation of mind to the state of the weather, it was sufficiently perceptible that their alarms also arose from a cause which they did not acknowledge.

"The lamp at the binnacle being re-lighted, they perceived that the ship lay closer to the wind than she had hitherto done, and the spirits of the passengers were somewhat revived.

"Nevertheless, neither the tempestuous state of the atmosphere nor the thunder had ceased; and soon a vivid flash of lightning showed the waves tumbling around us, and in the distance the ' Flying Dutchman scudding furiously before the wind, under a press of canvas. The sight was but momentary, but it was sufficient to remove all doubt from the minds of the passengers. One of the men cried aloud, 'There she goes, top-gallants and all!'

"The chaplain had brought up his prayer-book, in order that he might draw from thence something to fortify and tranquillise the minds of the rest. Therefore, taking his seat near the binnacle, so that the light shone upon the white leaves of the book, he, in a solemn tone, read out the service for those distressed at sea. The sailors stood round with folded arms, and looked as if they thought it would be of little use. But this served to occupy the attention of those on deck for a while.

" In the meantime, the flashes of lightning becoming less vivid, showed nothing else, far or near, but the billows weltering round the vessel. The sailors seemed to think that they had not yet seen the worst, but confined their remarks and prognostications to their own circle.

"At this time, the captain, who had hitherto remained in his berth, came on deck, and with a gay and unconcerned air, inquired what was the cause of the general dread. He said he thought they had already seen the worst of the weather, and wondered that his men had raised such a hubbub about a capful of wind. Mention being made of the 'Flying Dutchman,' the captain laughed. He said 'he would like very much to see any vessel carrying top-gallant sails in

such a night, for it would be a sight worth looking at.'
The chaplain taking him by one of the buttons of his
coat, drew ⸲ him aside, and appeared to enter into
serious conversation with him. While they were talking
together, the captain was heard to say, ' Let us look
to our own ship, and not mind such things '; and
accordingly, he sent a man aloft, to see if all was right
about the foretopsail yard, which was chafing the mast
with a loud noise. It was Tom Willis who went up;
and when he came down, he said that all was tight, and
that he hoped it would soon get clearer; and that they
would see no more of what they were most afraid of.

"The captain and first mate were heard laughing
loudly together, while the chaplain observed that it
would be better to repress such unseasonable gaiety.
The second mate, a native of Scotland, whose name
was Duncan Saunderson, having attended one of the
university classes at Aberdeen, thought himself too
wise to believe all that the sailors said, and took part
with the captain. He jestingly told Willis to borrow
his grandam's spectacles the next time he was sent to
keep a look-out ahead. Tom walked sulkily away,
muttering that he would nevertheless trust to his own
eyes till morning, and accordingly took his station at
the bow, and appeared to watch as attentively as
before.

"The sound of talking soon ceased, for many returned
to their berths ; and we heard nothing but the clank-

ing of the ropes upon the masts, and the bursting of
the billows ahead, as the vessel successively took the
seas.

"But after a considerable interval of darkness, gleams
of lightning began to reappear. Tom Willis suddenly
called out, 'Vanderdecken again! Vanderdecken
again! I see them letting down a boat.'

"All who were on deck ran to the bows. The next
flash of lightning shone far and wide over the raging
sea, and showed us, not only the 'Flying Dutchman' at
a distance, but also a boat coming from her with four
men. The boat was within two cables' length of our
ship's side.

"The man who first saw her ran to the captain and
asked whether they should hail her or not. The captain, walking about in great agitation, made no reply.
The first mate cried, 'Whose going to heave a rope to
that boat?' The men looked at each other without
offering to do anything. The boat had come very
near the chains, when Tom Willis called out, 'What
do you want? or what the devil has blown you here
in such weather?' A piercing voice from the boat
replied in English, 'We want to speak with your captain.' The captain took no notice of this, and Vanderdecken's boat having come close alongside, one of
the men came upon deck, and appeared like a fatigued
and weather-beaten seaman, holding some letters in his
hand.

"Our sailors all drew back. The chaplain, however, looking steadfastly upon him, went forward a few steps, and asked, ' What is the purpose of this visit ? '

"The stranger replied, 'We have long been kept here by foul weather, and Vanderdecken wishes to send these letters to his friends in Europe.'

"Our captain now came forward and said, as firmly as he could, 'I wish Vanderdecken would put his letters on board any vessel rather than mine.'

"The stranger replied, 'We have tried many a ship, but most of them refuse our letters.'

"Upon which Tom Willis muttered, 'It will be best for us if we do the same, for they say there is sometimes a sinking weight in your paper.'

"The stranger took no notice of this, but asked where we were from. On being told that we were from Portsmouth, he said, as with strong feeling, 'Would that you had rather been from Amsterdam! Oh that we saw it again! We must see our friends again.' When he uttered these words, the men who were in the boat below wrung their hands, and cried, in a piercing tone in Dutch, 'Oh that we saw it again! We have been long here beating about; but we must see our friends again ! '

"The chaplain asked the stranger, 'How long have you been at sea?' He replied, 'We have lost our count, for our almanack was blown overboard. Our ship, you see, is there still; so why should you ask how long we have been at sea? For Vanderdecken only wishes to write home and comfort his friends.'

"To which the chaplain replied, 'Your letters, I fear, would be of no use in Amsterdam even if they were delivered, for the persons to whom they are addressed are probably no longer to be found there, except under very ancient green turf in the churchyard.'

"The unwelcome stranger then wrung his hands and appeared to weep; and replied, 'It is impossible. We cannot believe you. We have been long driving about here, but country nor relations cannot be so easily forgotten. There is not a rain-drop in the air but feels itself kindred to all the rest, and they fall back into the sea to meet with each other again. How, then, can kindred blood be made to forget where it came from. Even our bodies are part of the ground of Holland; and Vanderdecken says, if he once were come to Amsterdam, he would rather be changed into a stone post, well fixed into the ground, than leave it again, if that were to die elsewhere. But in the meantime we only ask you to take these letters.'

"The chaplain, looking at him with astonishment, said, 'This is the insanity of natural affection which rebels against all measures of time and distance.'

"The stranger continued, 'Here is a letter from our second mate to his dear and only remaining friend, his uncle, the merchant who lives in the second house on Stuncken Yacht Quay.'

" He held forth the letter, but no one would approach to take it.

"Tom Willis raised his voice and said, ' One of our men here says that he was in Amsterdam last summer, and he knows for certain that the street called Stuncken Yacht Quay was pulled down sixty years ago, and now there is only a large church at that place.'

" The man from the ' Flying Dutchman ' said, ' It is impossible; we cannot believe you. Here is another letter from myself, in which I have sent a bank-note to my dear sister, to buy some gallant lace, to make her a high head-dress.'

" Tom Willis, hearing this, said, ' It is most likely that her head now lies under a tombstone, which will outlast all the changes of fashion. But on what house is your bank-note ? '

" The stranger replied, ' On the house of Vander-brucker and Company.'

" The man of whom Tom Willis had spoken said, ' I guess there will now be some discount upon it, for that banking-house has gone to destruction some forty years ago; and Vanderbrucker was afterwards missing. But to remember these things is like raking up the bottom of an old canal.'

" The stranger called passionately, ' It is impossible ! we cannot believe it. It is cruel to say such things to people in our condition. There is a letter from our captain himself to his much-beloved and faithful wife, whom he left at a pleasant summer dwelling on the border of the Haarlemer Mer. She promised to have the house beautifully painted and gilded before he came back, and to get a new set of looking-glasses for the principal chamber, that she might see as many images of Vanderdecken as if she had six husbands at once.'

" The man replied, ' There has been time enough for her to have had six husbands since then; but were she alive still, there is no fear that Vanderdecken would ever get home to disturb her.'

"On hearing this the stranger again shed tears, and said if they would not take the letters, he would leave them; and looking around, he offered the parcel to the captain, chaplain, and to the rest of the crew successively. But each drew back as it was offered, and put his hands behind his back. He then laid the letters upon the deck, and placed upon them a piece of iron, which was lying near, to prevent them from being blown away. Having done this, he swung himself over the gangway, and went into the boat.

" We heard the others speak to him, but the rise of a sudden squall prevented us from distinguishing his reply. The boat was seen to quit the ship's side, and in a few moments there were no more traces of her than if she had never been there. The sailors rubbed their eyes, as if doubting what they had witnessed; but the parcel still lay upon deck, and proved the reality of all that had passed.

"Duncan Saunderson, the Scotch mate, asked the captain if he should take them up and put them in the letter-bag. Receiving no reply, he would have lifted them if it had not been for Tom Willis, who pulled him back, saying that nobody should touch them.

"In the meantime the captain went down to the cabin; and the chaplain, having followed him, found him at his bottle-case, pouring out a large dram of brandy. The captain, although somewhat disconcerted, immediately offered the glass to him, saying, 'Here, Charters, is what is good in a cold night.' The chaplain declined drinking anything, and the captain having swallowed the bumper, they both returned to the deck, where they found the seamen giving their opinions concerning what should be done with the letters. Tom Willis proposed to pick them up on a harpoon and throw it overboard.

"Another speaker said, 'I have always heard it asserted that it is neither safe to accept them voluntarily, nor, when they are left, to throw them out of the ship.'

"'Let no one touch them,' said the carpenter. 'The way to do with the letters from the Flying Dutchman is to case them upon deck by nailing boards over them, so that if he sends back for them, they are still there to give him.'

"The carpenter went to fetch his tools. During his

absence the ship gave so violent a pitch that the piece
of iron slid off the letters, and they were whirled overboard by the wind, like birds of evil omen whirring
through the air. There was a cry of joy among the
sailors, and they ascribed the favourable change which
soon took place in the weather to our having got quit
of Vanderdecken. We soon got under weigh again.
The night-watch being set, the rest of the crew retired
to their berths."

If Herr Wagner owes much to Mdlle. Albani, who,
by her impersonations of Elsa in *Lohengrin*, of Elizabeth in *Tannhäuser*, and of Senta in the *Flying Dutchman*, has helped more than any other artist to ensure
the success of his works in England, Mdlle. Albani is,
on her side, much indebted to Herr Wagner, whose
creations inspire her with a poetical enthusiasm such as
never could have been awakened in her breast by the
conventional heroines of the ordinary operatic drama.
Opera-books are not, as a rule, written by poets. They
are put together by playwrights, more or less ingenious;
or, rather, by literary carpenters, whose only ambition
is to construct a suitable framework which the composer, like a musical upholsterer, may decorate with
airs, ducts, concerted pieces, and finales. Such a process of construction takes no account of character;
nor, under such conditions, would the creation and
development of character be possible. Accordingly,
operatic heroines are all cast in one mould, or at most

in two—the light soprano mould from which have issued Elvira, Linda, Lucia; and the heavy or dramatic soprano mould which has turned out Norma, Lucrezia Borgia, and Semiramide. Semiramis, Lucrezia Borgia, and Norma, as represented on the operatic stage, are not simply members of the same family, not merely sisters, but one and the same person dressed now as an Assyrian queen, now as a Venetian lady, now as a Druidical priestess. Yet surely Norma and Lucrezia, Norma and Semiramide, have nothing in common? Not in the dramas to which these personages originally belonged; but only in the lyrical dramas to which they have since been transferred—bound by operatic requirements and fettered by operatic traditions. The main difference between the light soprano and the dramatic soprano, in respect to temperament, is that the latter, when she gets into trouble, becomes enraged, and tries to injure some one, whereas the former loses her spirits and sinks into a gentle insanity. Three light soprano characters, taken at random, have been mentioned, and all three behave in the manner just stated. Nor are Elvira, Lucia, and Linda exceptional personages. The exceptional personage in serious opera is the light soprano who does *not* go mad—as, for instance, Gilda in *Rigoletto*. Martha, in the opera of that name, only abstains from becoming insane because Lionel, the tenor, saves her the trouble by becoming insane in her place. Catherine, in *L'Etoile du Nord*, is crazy from the beginning almost to the end of the third act; Dinorah is, throughout the opera to which she gives her name, as mad as the proverbial March hare, and she becomes madder still after the climax at the end of the second act—that critical juncture at which the reason of nine heroines, of the "light" order, out of ten gives way. The ordinary operatic heroine trusts in the first act, is deceived in the second, and goes mad in the third. She is without character, and is remembered not as an individual, but as a member of a large and uninteresting class of melodious lunatics.

What a contrast to this colourless personage does the Wagnerian heroine present! For, with many points of difference, the heroines of Wagner's operas undoubtedly resemble one another by certain fundamental characteristics, such as nobility of disposition and elevation of thought. They are at once delicate and strong; their innocence being to them what bodily integrity is to Lohengrin, who, if he loses the least particle of flesh, is at the mercy of his enemies, but as long as he remains intact is unconquerable. Elsa, Elizabeth, Senta are all fearless, and Senta is the most fearless of them all. Elsa consents to share Lohengrin's mysterious fate, and desires for his sake to bear half the burden of his unutterable secret. Elizabeth, carried away by the passionate eloquence of Tannhäuser, defies the opinion of those stern ascetics, Wolfram and his brother bards — in its way as great a proof of courage, and as commendable a one, as a woman could give. Senta, however, is more daring than either Elizabeth or Elsa, and the life of which she desires to partake is surrounded by terrors which are not only mysterious but also real and perfectly appreciable. Elsa had faith in the advent of a deliverer before Lohengrin actually appeared; and Senta, long before the Flying Dutchman came into her presence as a living being, had been haunted by the legend of his sufferings, and by his sorrowful countenance as portrayed in the picture at which she is perpetually gazing. Thus, Senta's mood, when the Flying Dutchman first stands before her, is much the same as Elsa's mood when Lohengrin suddenly arrives. Without expecting him, she is full of his image. He comes to her, moreover, in the character of a deliverer; for he saves her, not indeed from the attacks of calumny, but from the wearisome persecutions of a prosaic love. Like Elsa and like Elizabeth, this pure, spiritual, and courageous heroine is ready at any moment to lay down her life for the one man to whom she is devoted; though, as a matter of fact, Senta sacrifices herself unconsciously. When the Dutchman sails away she throws herself into the sea simply from despair at his refusing to let her share his terrible existence, and without any knowledge of the conditions under which he is condemned to wander on the ocean until he shall meet with a woman "faithful unto death." The

I. 14

spell is broken by means which the devil himself had not foreseen, and of which the contrivance is due to the more than diabolical ingenuity of Heinrich Heine.

As regards the sources of Wagner's *Flying Dutchman* libretto, the pages devoted to the subject by Dr. Hueffer in his "Music of the Future," may be profitably consulted; though it would seem that neither Dr. Hueffer nor anyone else can trace the legend of the "Flying Dutchman" further back than a number of "Blackwood's Magazine" published in 1821. Quite different from the general run of operas by its subject, or rather by its poetical treatment, the *Flying Dutchman* bears a greater resemblance to the works of the ordinary operatic composer than does either *Lohengrin* or even *Tannhäuser*, its immediate successor. Herr Wagner has explained, for the benefit of those who had misunderstood him, that he did not invent his theory of the musical drama first and write operas to suit it afterwards. He developed his system spontaneously and half-unconsciously, and had finished and produced on the stage those works by which he is at this moment best known before he published his treatises on "Opera and Drama" and on the "Art-work of the Future." In the *Flying Dutchman* there are a certain number of striking, symmetrical tunes; though most play-goers and opera-goers not yet reconciled to Wagner's music will think that in the first act there is a superabundance of recitative. Descriptive and suggestive phrases, fragments of phrases, and melodic passages of the briefest kind paint the atmosphere of sea and storm in which the first act takes place. The pilot sings something very like a song, and the sailors forget themselves so far as to break into a highly rhythmical chorus, which, however, they soon discontinue. There is not, on the whole, much abuse of dance-forms, not much robbery of the "people's melody" in the first act of the *Flying Dutchman*. The second act, however, is quite operatic, in the usual sense of the word. It contains a spinning chorus which is not only beautiful, like so much that Wagner has produced, but one might almost say "pretty"; a legendary ballad in two verses which might, in a happy moment, have been written by more than one popular operatic composer of the day; and a duet for Senta and her lover of every-day life, which, though by no means open to the charge of being common-place, might have occurred in any of the conventional operas—operas, that is to say, in the received forms—that Herr Wagner now so strongly condemns.

The "leading motive" system is but sparingly employed in the *Flying Dutchman*. Four significant notes, however, on the horn have the effect from time to time of recalling the figure of the Dutchman and the ballad on the subject of his fate sung by Senta. Of course Mdlle. Albani sings the ballad as perfectly

14 *

and expressively as it can be sung. M. Maurel, too, is
most impressive and most interesting as the Flying
Dutchman—a weird, fantastic, and truly mysterious
personage, exciting terror in most natures, but pity,
sympathy, and love in the hearts of those who, like
Senta, can understand him. In Senta's ballad, by
the way, the chorus is unduly and too frequently emphatic. It has a right to be frightened by Senta's
story, but not by every word and every syllable that
she utters.

It need not now be set forth for the hundredth time
how the *Flying Dutchman* is no fair specimen of that
" art work " with which Herr Wagner proposes to
endow the " future" Opera-goers, too, have already
been sufficiently reminded that this, the first of its
composer's works which fairly took hold of the public,
has been discarded by its own creator. Herr Wagner
cannot, however, by taking thought make himself either
greater or less than he really is ; and the *Flying Dutchman*, though composed and produced some thirty years
before the famous Trilogy was completed, belongs to
its author, and is as characteristic of his genius as any
and everything else that has proceeded from his pen.
In England, where neither *Lohengrin* nor *Tannhäuser*
has been unappreciated, *Der Fliegende Holländer* ought
to meet with as large an amount of favour as has
fallen to the lot of the two later works. Nor is it
unlikely that, even in Germany, *Der Fliegende Halländer*

will, at the very least, keep its position by the side of the operas composed in Herr Wagner's second and third styles. If to enrich his country with a series of thoroughly German works was Herr Wagner's object, he has certainly reached his aim in the case of the *Flying Dutchman,* which is as German as *Der Freischütz* itself. It is based, indeed, on just such a romantic legend as Weber might have loved to treat. The melodies, too, in which it abounds, if not by any means imitated from Weber, seem here and there to have been inspired by the genius of the admirable composer whom Herr Wagner somewhere speaks of as "my venerated master." Long singable passages are much more numerous in the *Flying Dutchman* than in any other of Herr Wagner's works—with the exception, perhaps, of *Rienzi,* until lately unknown in England. Of "leading motives," on the other hand, marking with a musical stamp principal personages, fundamental incidents, and everything that is meant to be striking in the drama, we have but one example—the four mysterious notes given out by one or more of the wind instruments whenever the Flying Dutchman appears, or is mentioned, or may be supposed to pass as an idea through the mind of one of the characters on the stage. In the four parts of the prologue and Trilogy performed at Baireuth something like ninety "leading motives" have been discovered, taken out of the score, and printed by themselves; and such helps to memory will be indispensable if the Wagnerian system of composition, as lately perfected by the inventor, should ever become general.

CHAPTER XXI.

TANNHÄUSER.

Composed some years earlier than *Lohengrin, Tannhäuser* still resembles, in many respects, the ordinary
opera—a resemblance which becomes fainter and fainter
as Herr Wagner advances in his career, until at last
we find him significantly abandoning the name of
" opera," and describing his musical dramas by the
vague title of " performances." The Wagnerian system
admits, or at one time did admit, the use of measured
music, in the shape of what are ordinarily called
" tunes," for marches and choruses ; and in *Tannhäuser*
airs, distinctly recognisable as such, occur even in the
solo parts. The second act, too, closes with something
very like a concerted finale. *Tannhäuser,* in short, is
the work of a musical knight, who, like Tannhäuser

himself, had passed long days and nights on the
Venusberg, and who, when he wrote the work in question, had not quite liberated himself from the seductive influence of " melody," as the word is generally
understood. Tannhäuser had a lurking suspicion
almost to the last that there was more in the Venusberg philosophy than those champions of asceticism,
Wolfram, Walther, and Biterholf, had any notion of.
But he undertook the pilgrimage to Rome all the
same; and when everyone has made the pilgrimage to
Baireuth there will, perhaps, be a general conversion
on the part of lovers of music from a taste for tune to
a toleration more or less sincere of dignified tuneless-
ness. As a drama, independently of the musical setting, *Tannhäuser* is altogether admirable. The subject
is symbolical, both in its general conception and as
Herr Wagner has treated it, in all its details. Herr
Wagner's preference for legendary subjects is well
known, and his special liking for them is justified by
the striking results he attains when he presents them
in dramatic form. The knight Tannhäuser, with a
Christian love for Elizabeth, niece of the Landgrave
of Thuringia, entertains a pagan love for Venus, who
entices him to the Venusberg, where, like so many
other knights, ancient and modern—like Ulysses in
the island of Calypso, like Hannibal at Capua, and
like Nelson at Naples—he remains for a time forgetful
of his highest duties. Ulysses, as Mr. Lewes has

pointed out in a very interesting passage in his " Life of Goethe," on the significance of the Faust legend— left his Calypso (*" qui ne pouvait se consoler du départ d'Ulysse "*), and went about his business as if nothing had happened. Tannhäuser, however, felt that, by remaining on the Venusberg, he had rendered himself guilty of mortal sin. The anonymous author of the most ancient version of the Faust legend requests his readers to repeat to themselves, in connection with Faust's sale of his own soul, these lines :—

> Who of the future takes no heed,
> But only thinks of present need,
> The devil has him in his hold;
> By day and night the man is sold.

According to this view, Tannhäuser also was sold to the devil; and the Tannhäuser of the legend does, in fact, address Venus, his so-called " wife," as *" eine Teufelinn."* Tannhäuser has been drawn to the devil —or to Venus—by his own superior artistic qualities. It does not fall to the lot of everyone to go to the Venusberg; and neither Wolfram nor Walther nor the peculiarly stern Biterholf would have been likely to find their way there. At least, Venus would not have tempted them as she did Tannhäuser, whom, in the first scene of Wagner's beautiful opera, we find subjected, willingly enough, to all the blandishments of which the Queen of Love can dispose.

According to the design of Herr Wagner, who does

nothing by halves, the stage, in the opening scene, should be adorned with representations of mythical and symbolical amours, such as the famous one between Leda and Jupiter. Nymphs in various stages of excitement disport themselves around the entranced warrior. A troop of bacchantes urge them to renewed exertions, and in the distance the voices of sirens are heard calling upon the knight to give himself up to love and pleasure. When the excitement is at its height, " weariness and torpor," in the words of the stage direction, " seize the dancers." The groups of bacchantes disappear at the back, whence arises " a rosy vapour," which gradually spreads over the entire stage, covering nymphs and sirens, and at last leaving no one visible but Venus and Tannhäuser, who are reclining in the foreground. The chorus of sirens is still heard. But nymphs and bacchantes are now reposing under the influence of " rosy vapour "—which may be regarded as symbolical for red wine and for sensual delights generally—and the song of the sirens has a " dying fall," until, little by little, it becomes inaudible. Then Tannhäuser awakens as from a dream, while Venus " draws him towards her caressingly." For a moment the knight covers his eyes with his hands as if to retain the impression of a beautiful vision, and then, in the customary Wagnerian recitative, gives Venus to understand that he has had enough of this sort of thing ; that for days and months he has been living in an enchanted palace in the midst of ballet-dancing and blue lights, and that the time has now come for him to look once more upon the outer world, breathe fresh air, inhale the fragrance of flowers, and listen to the songs of birds. Venus seeks to retain him, assuring him that peace and contentment are not to be found in earthly struggles, and that she alone is the fountain of true happiness. Tannhäuser, who from time to time has lyrical outbursts, vows in one of these moments of expansion that his heart has been too much touched by Venus for him ever to forget her; that he will sing her praises before all men; but that he must do so as a free agent, and that he will no longer remain her slave.

Poor Tannhäuser is constantly troubled by the alternate promptings of a voluptuous temperament and of an exalted soul. But he escapes from Venus. He has no sooner pronounced his unalterable determination than her enchantments disappear. The knight now lies exhausted in a valley full of the natural sights and sounds for which his better nature had longed. Sheep-bells are heard, and a shepherd plays and sings to the accompaniment of his pipe a symbolical song which is *naïveté* itself, and, as such, in striking contrast with the elaborately seductive strains heard in the heated atmosphere of Venus's court. The mysterious mountain where the goddess resides is still seen in the distance. So also is the Castle of Wartburg, from which

a road, passing by a shrine of the Holy Virgin, leads
to the valley. Down this path pilgrims are descending. They pray as they march slowly along; and
Tannhäuser, roused by the sound of their voices, falls
on his knees and joins in their song of repentance.
When the pilgrims have passed away, and nothing is
heard but the distant sound of their voices and of the
bells of the church towards which they are directing
their steps, the unhappy Tannhäuser has a temporary
relapse. He sinks to the ground, but has not been
long in the dust when the Landgrave of Thuringia
arrives with a number of " bards " or minnesingers,
who, recognising in the fallen figure an acquaintance
and an associate, raise him up, endeavour to console
him, but cannot reconcile him to existence until at
last Wolfram utters the name of Elizabeth. At the
thought of this Christian maiden the late worshipper
of Venus consents to return to his friends, in the hope,
apparently, that " all will be forgotten." The " bards "
mount their steeds and sound their horns; and amid
the echoing and re-echoing of horns, and to the sound
of a spirited chorus from the bards, the curtain comes
down.

The first act is not merely an introduction to the
second and third. It contains within itself the germs
of the other two. Thus Tannhäuser has sworn on all
occasions to do befitting honour to the name of Venus,
and in a competition of bards for supremacy in lyric

poetry, with the divine Elizabeth as prize, Venus's faithful servant and former slave breaks into an impassioned celebration of her mystic virtues, which the gentle Elizabeth, with the fire of love in her heart, is inclined to applaud until she is interrupted by three indignant bards, who explain how wrong it is, and, to mark their sense of its impropriety, propose to put Tannhäuser to death. The matter is compromised by the substitution of pilgrimage for capital punishment; and it is understood, at the end of the second act, that the knight who had surrendered himself to enchantments and pleasures of the senses, is going as a penitent to Rome.

Venus, however, had warned her lover that he would find neither peace nor forgiveness in the world; and the Pope equally tells him that there is no remission for his sin, and that after his life on the Venusberg it is as impossible for him to become a new man as for his pilgrim's staff to put forth new leaves. In his despair Tannhäuser turns once more to Venus, always ready to receive him. But Wolfram adjures him, in the name of Elizabeth—who has died of grief on learning that forgiveness was denied him—not to show himself unworthy of her love. With a prayer to "Saint Elizabeth" to intercede for him, the much-tried knight expires; and as he yields his last breath a band of young pilgrims arrive, bearing, in token of his pardon, the staff which he had carried to Rome, now

covered with green leaves! A chorus of thanksgiving
is heard. The sun rises above the fatal mountain.
Purity has triumphed over impurity; and a highly
poetical work, with deep significance in every incident
and scene, full of dramatic emotion, full also of picturesque and spectacular beauties, is at an end.

The opera is admirably proportioned, the action goes
on continuously, each scene leading logically to the
scene succeeding it, and the interest is confined to
four characters, and among these concentrated in two:
Tannhäuser, the well-intentioned and high-minded but
guilty knight; and Elizabeth, the pure-hearted maiden,
whose sole aspiration is that her lover may obtain the
forgiveness of heaven—she, in the fulness of her affection, having at once pardoned him. Mdlle. Albani is
seen and heard in this most interesting character to as
much advantage as in that of Elsa. In the second act
she is brilliant, animated; and in the final scene, where
Tannhäuser starts on his pilgrimage, very dramatic.
In the third act, however, she reaches still higher
ground; and in the scene where, unable to find Tannhäuser among the pilgrims who have received absolution, she gives expression to her grief in a prayer to
the Virgin, Mddle. Albani sings the beautiful melody
with a purity and pathos which those who have once
heard her will never forget. The saddened Elizabeth
of the third act is in strong contrast with the joyous
Elizabeth of the second, of whose impulsive nature,

however, traces are to be found in the religious fervour of the heart-broken young girl.

It would be difficult to cull from *Tannhäuser* one of those "bouquets of melodies" which are yielded so plentifully to pianoforte arrangers by the popular Italian, French, and even German operas of the last half-century. But compare it, not to *Semiramide*, *Lucrezia Borgia*, *Norma*, and *Il Trovatore*—with which it has nothing in common—but to the *Preciosa* and *Euryanthe* of Weber, and it is not so very unlike works whose claims to be regarded as operas have never been denied. When Herr Wagner is melodious he is melodious after the manner of Weber; and Wolfram's address to the evening star, at the moment of Elizabeth's death, is somewhat in the style of that most poetical composer. The march, again, is quite Weberian, the principal motive being not merely inspired by, but, consciously or unconsciously, borrowed from the last movement of Agatha's air in *Der Freischütz*. The most original and by far the most graceful melody in *Tannhäuser* is the prayer to the Virgin, sung with admirable purity of expression by Mdlle. Albani; and here, at least, the accompaniments—in most places brassy and overpowering—are appropriately subdued. For once Herr Wagner has "tempered the wind," not to the shorn lamb, but to the wounded dove; so that the heart-broken Elizabeth is at liberty to breathe forth her prayer in the most delicate pianissimo, with the certainty (when her enunciation is as perfect as is that of Mdlle. Albani) that her utterances will not be rendered inaudible by the blasting of trumpets and trombones.

Herr Wagner's poverty as an inventor of melodies is shown very conspicuously, and greatly to the damage of his work considered as a drama, in two places : in the first act, where the strains assigned to the Goddess of Love are neither voluptuous nor in any sense delightful, and in the contest between the bards in Act II., where the champions of Platonic love and the disciple of Venus are equally tedious, and tedious in precisely the same style. A Rossini would at least have shown himself equal to the musical demands of the Venusberg; and a Meyerbeer would probably not have neglected— or, rather, would have been able to turn to account—the opportunities for contrast afforded by the very different sentiments which the impressionable Tannhäuser on the one hand, and his ascetic friends on the other, profess on the subject of Woman and the way to treat her. Schumann was of opinion that Wagner would have been the greatest composer of his time had he possessed the gift of melody—rather an important proviso; and his deficiencies in the matter of tunefulness not only leave his works in a great measure barren of charm, but render it impossible for him to introduce into them such opposition of light and shade as the subjects, and Herr Wagner's own manner of regarding them, would seem to invite. In a mediæval legendary romance like

Tannhäuser trivial dance-tunes would, of course, be out of place. It is not necessary either that Tannhäuser should sing a brindisi or that Venus should dance the cancan. But the airs of the Venusberg ought to be, as far as possible, of a fascinating character; and the *Laus Veneris* of Tannhäuser should be full of abandonment.

Herr Wagner is more successful in giving a musical physiognomy to the noble, self-sacrificing Wolfram, and to the pure-minded, saint-like Elizabeth, than in painting by means of tones the enchantress Venus or that complex character Tannhäuser—now a reckless voluptuary, now a weeping penitent. The spiritually incomplete Tannhäuser has, of course, greater charms for the gentle but impulsive Elizabeth than are possessed by the evenly developed Wolfram. If Wolfram is the more virtuous man, Tannhäuser ¦is the better poet; and though Tannhäuser does not love Elizabeth after the manner prescribed by Wolfram, Bitterolf, and the rest of the noble company of bards, he loves her as she wishes to be loved. Bitterolf, knowing that Elizabeth cares nothing for him nor for anyone but Tannhäuser, would like her to be loved calmly and at a distance. Not so Elizabeth herself. But she at once subordinates her affectionate impulses to her sense of duty and of religion; and the whole nature of this charming heroine — so different from the ordinary operatic heroine who gushes in the first act and goes

I. 15

mad in the third—is shown in the scene of Tannhäuser's departure for Rome, where Elizabeth, grieving
to lose him, gives him in the tenderest manner her
blessing, while he, always abject, kneels down and
devours the hem of her garment with his kisses.
The opera abounds in pictures, of which Elizabeth
blessing Tannhäuser as he starts on his pilgrimage,
Elizabeth praying to the Virgin as she awaits the
pilgrim's return, and Elizabeth going up the mountain-
side to die, are the three most beautiful; while the
most magnificent is the procession and assembly of
courtiers in the scene of the minstrels' competition.
There is not much picturesqueness about Tannhäuser
personally; but he has characteristic attitudes, and one
cannot but think of him as in a kneeling or in a recumbent position. In the first act we see him lying on the
ground, exhausted by the orgies of the Venusberg.
In the second act he prostrates himself before Elizabeth
in token of misbehaviour, repentance, and supplication.
In the third act, penitent but unabsolved, he crawls on
to tell his sorrows to Wolfram and to proclaim, in the
spirit of cynicism bred by remorse, that his only hope
now is in abandonment to pleasure; while at the close
of the third act, when the dead body of Elizabeth is
carried down from the mountain, he stretches himself
out at full length on the ground beside the bier,
covered with flowers, on which her companions have
placed her, and in this position expires. Very different

is the demeanour of the virtuous and self-possessed Wolfram from that of Tannhäuser. Wolfram is always firm and erect. Elizabeth, on her part, is more than erect; she is aspiring. She elevates herself by prayer, she mounts to a higher sphere even as she ascends the mountain on which she dies; and she takes her place in heaven just as the evening star, so significantly addressed by Wolfram, appears in the sky.

CHAPTER XXII.

LOHENGRIN.

A KING, two knights (one good, the other bad), a
virtuous princess, a wicked enchantress, a swan, and
a dove are the active personages in this drama, which
introduces three states of ecstasy, including two visions;
several miracles (including one miraculous transformation), one tournament, one attempt at murder, one death
from stabbing, three marches, four grand pageants, and
five horses. The piece is full of tumult, picturesqueness, character, and colour. All that is pure in the
play is presented in symbolical white. The miraculous
swan, the mystic dove, are, of course, white. The
girlish little lad into whom the swan is ultimately
changed, or rather retransformed, shines ·in white
armour and whiter silk. Lohengrin wears a silver

helmet, surmounted by a silver swan, carries a silver shield, is encased in silver armcur, and has nothing un-silvery about him but his little horn of gold, and a black heart-shaped escutcheon on his breast, from which stands out an emblematic swan—once more in silver. Elsa, the typical maiden of ancient ballads, suffering under foul calumny, but spotless as snow, is clad in white, in white and silver, and in white and gold. The King, too, rides a white horse, which Wagner would not have allowed him to do if he had not intended to show that he considered him a good king at heart. The bad characters, on the other hand, are ill dressed in dark brown or in dull red. The vile Frederic of Telramund is exhibited in the garb of a beggar; and the wicked Ortrud flaunts about in crimson and spangles.

Whatever else it may be, *Lohengrin* is not dull. Apart from the beauty of much of the music and from the general interest of the drama, it is full of passages which strike the eye, the heart, the imagination, or all three together. Nothing can be grander than the combination of sights and sounds in the scene where, while a procession of soldiers in gorgeous uniforms and priests in the brightest of robes moves across the stage in the midst of a crowd waving branches on all sides, the ringing of church bells and the pealing of the cathedral organ are heard simultaneously with the varied tones of the many-voiced orchestra. This and other scenes like it in an opera which abounds in

pageantry may render *Lohengrin* open to the charge of
sensationalism—for the amount of pure art which goes
to the composition of such scenes is very small. But
there are also scenes of the greatest simplicity for Elsa,
for Lohengrin, and for Elsa and Lohengrin together;
scenes which are full of emotion, and which, apart
from scenery, and with the commonest costumes, could
not but affect the listener. *Lohengrin* is, in fact, a
highly poetical melodrama, in which the mystical and
the actual are strangely blended together, though not
more strangely, perhaps, than in some of the plays of
Shakspeare and of the great Spanish dramatists.
It is full of the most delicate subtleties and of the
most palpable realities : fights on the stage and sugges-
tions of spiritual influences ; overpowering blasts of
trombones and luminous apparitions ; real horses in the
Astley's style, and visions of miraculous troops of angels.
Liszt's rhapsodical description of one of the most
striking scenes of the opera—that of Elsa's bridal procession, to which Wagner has composed music worthy
of Weber and quite in Weber's style—may be quoted
as an example of the sort of enthusiasm with which
Wagner in his best moments inspires his most fanatical
admirers. "During this scene," says Liszt, "Elsa
reappears at her balcony, and passes along the galleries
of the palace before descending to the street. Behind
her slowly passes a long cortège to music of a soft but
earnest character, admirably in keeping with the ap-

proaching religious ceremonial. Trembling with emotion, the Princess advances, looking more lovely than ever in her crown and silver-mounted robes. The passionate strains of the orchestra are inspired at once by love and devotion, but so mingled that it is impossible to discriminate between the two. The Princess, at once a saint and a woman, walks with downcast eyes; yet the strains of the music seem to reveal her thoughts, and in the vague mystic ardour of its majestic crescendo we may read how burning and yet how chaste are the glances which are concealed beneath the drooping eyelids." This is, of course, extravagant. But it seems less extravagant when one has seen *Lohengrin* at the Royal Italian Opera, and Mdlle. Albani as Elsa. Elsa is the soul of the work—or, perhaps, it would be juster to say the heart and soul of the work are Lohengrin and Elsa together.

The grief of Elsa, falsely accused, her ecstatic vision, and the mysterious arrival of Lohengrin; Elsa's prayer and Lohengrin's victory (in Act I.), Elsa's bridal procession (in Act II.); the orchestral introduction and bridal chorus; the duet for Lohengrin and Elsa, and finally Lohengrin's declaration, farewell, and departure (in Act III.) are the scenes and incidents which chiefly stamp themselves on the memory. If we also remember the singing of Ortrud and of Frederic, singly and together, it is to wish we had not heard it. The vocal utterances of these diabolical personages are obviously

intended to contrast with and to enhance the beauty of
the melodious phrases assigned to the angelic couple,
Lohengrin and Elsa. Set to music as Herr Wagner
has set them, the cries of the false knight and of
the malicious enchantress who is urging him on his
villainous course suggest not the wicked so much as
the wearisome. The so-called singing of this objectionable couple is both harsh and tedious, and about
half the second act is filled with it. Is it absolutely
necessary that bad characters should sing bad music?
Probably not. Bertram in *Robert le Diable,* Mephistopheles in *Faust,* sing melodies which are no doubt of a
sinister character, but which are melodies all the same.
Kaspar, again, in *Der Freischütz* is at once tuneful and
grotesque. Ortrud and Frederic, however, seem to be,
not singing, but grumbling and grunting, spitting,
cursing, and swearing in music; which is neither nice
nor necessary. To Elsa and to Lohengrin the composer, as of right, gave his best. To Ortrud and
Frederic, however, he has given neither his best music
nor his worst. He has not given them music at all,
but only certain unmusical sequences of musical sounds.
The duet between Ortrud and Frederic at the beginning
of the long second act is something terrible. The succeeding duet between Ortrud and Elsa is a little better
by reason of the passages for Elsa. But Ortrud's
defiance and Frederic's accusation in the same interminable act are odious.

Wagner's orchestration is known to be one of his
strong points; and the various combinations of instruments, which are often made not for their own sake
but to serve from time to time as characteristic accompaniment to the personages on the stage, produce their
effect upon audiences of all kinds even at a first representation. It has now become the rule at our lyrical
theatres—rule more honoured in the observance than
in the breach—to encore nothing in a Wagnerian
opera. But at the first performance of *Lohengrin* in
England, the soft, spiritual prelude to Act I. and the
vigorous quasi-martial prelude to Act III. were both
encored. Elsa was also compelled to repeat her beautiful prayer—obviously a mistake from a Wagnerian point
of view, since by the Wagnerian doctrine all " repeats "
are forbidden; and Lohengrin had to arrive twice over,
for the sake of the wonderful orchestral rush by which
his approach is indicated. This was clearly absurd.
But a great deal of what a mad doctor might call
" furor Teutonicus " was raging in the galleries; and it
seemed probable enough at one time that every piece,
or rather every distinguishable beauty in every scene,
would be redemanded. Yet some of the finest things
even in the first act, when admiration was fresh and
fervent, had to be passed over. It was impossible, for
instance, to call upon Mdlle. Albani to give a second
time the eloquent outburst of gratitude and joy with
which poor Elsa hails the victory of her champion,

the Knight of the Swan, over 'Frederic, her accuser.
This was one of Mdlle. Albani's most dramatic points
—though it is not for particular points here and there,
but for her general conception of the part, that she
deserves praise. The fair-haired heroine of the mediæval legend, calm under calumny, strong in her innocence, full of devotion to her deliverer, but urged by a
fatal curiosity to put to him the question which he
must not answer, is perfectly represented by this admirable artist, whose voice, moreover, gives melody to
phrases which are not always in themselves melodious.
Mdlle. Albani had had the advantage of studying the
part of Elsa under Herr Wüllner, the Kapellmeister
of the Court Theatre at Munich; and to his intelligent
and careful instruction much of her success in this
difficult but far from ungrateful character may doubtless
be attributed.

The moral of *Lohengrin* seems to be that if a husband
treats his wife well she should not be too inquisitive
about his private affairs, apart from her; and also that
to be able to resist his enemies a man must be
perfect at all points. Lohengrin, if he loses one atom
of his flesh, will be at the mercy of everyone. Let
him, however, preserve his bodily integrity and he may
defy attacks from all sides. This can only mean that
the true knight, like Lohengrin, must be careful of his
honour. Once touched, it is gone. *Lohengrin*, however, may be viewed in a great many different lights:

as an opera in the ordinary sense of the word, as a spectacular piece, as an interesting drama, and as a sort of
miracle play, full of *naïveté*, quaintness, and symbolism
of all kinds. No one who is capable of taking an
interest in things dramatic can fail to be moved by it
in some way; and most persons must carry away from
its representation a deep impression of its beauty. If
we except the well-known introduction to the third act,
with its vigorous melody for trombones accompanied
by a twittering of violins; the graceful music of Elsa's
bridal procession, which is "tuneful" in the ordinary
sense of the word; and the thoroughly beautiful "prelude," none of the *Lohengrin* music ought ever to be
heard apart from the drama to which it belongs. But
the work, as a whole, is very effective, and Elsa
and Lohengrin are the two most poetical figures
of the modern stage. Were it not for the prelude,
which is a significant melodic epitome of all that is
most poetical and most essential in the work, the
way to enjoy *Lohengrin* would be to enter the
theatre as Elsa enters upon the stage. We should
thus have the satisfaction of escaping the oppressive
declamation of Henry the Fowler, of his Herald or
Town Crier, of Telramund, and of Ortrud; and could
listen with almost unmixed delight to the magic strains
associated with Elsa and Lohengrin. Groanings,
blasphemies, and curses such as the bad characters in
Lohengrin seem to be constantly vomiting forth are not

only offensive but in the end fatiguing. One can appreciate the purity of Elsa and the nobility of Lohengrin without having their opposites thrust perpetually, as if by way of contrast, before us. But start from the entry of Elsa; and from that point to the end of the act—including Elsa's prayer and vision, the arrival of Lohengrin, with its tumultuous choral and orchestral accompaniment, Lohengrin's farewell to the Swan, Lohengrin's brief declaration of love, and the stirring concerted finale—everything is admirable. Indeed, the passages given to Lohengrin and Elsa, either directly for the voice or indirectly in symphonic form, are full of melodious beauty and so appropriate to the personages that they seem to hang around them like a musical atmosphere.

There are already as many editions of this eminently modern work as of nearly all the great literary classics of antiquity. There is a Munich edition with " cuts," tenderly executed by Herr Wüllner, who is nothing if not a Wagnerian. There is a Berlin version, in which excisions of a more thorough-going kind have been practised. Then there is a *Lohengrin* as prepared for the use of New Yorkers. There is the Covent Garden *Lohengrin*, in which the cuts and compressions of Munich have, I believe, been adopted, but carried further than Herr Wüllner had the heart to go with them ; and finally, there is a Majesty's Theatre *Lohengrin*, in which Sir Michael Costa has slashed the work in heroic style—treating it, in fact, as St. Michael treated the Dragon. Before drawing the dragon's teeth, Sir Michael Costa is understood to have addressed himself to the proper authority for permission. In these cases, as when a public character is asked to say whether he would like to be caricatured and held up to the ridicule of the mob, it is usual to reply in polite language: "Don't mind me, and while you are about it pray do your worst." In the good old days of the hatchet and the block, the executioner used to ask pardon of the victim before taking his head off; and when a composer about to be "cut" is asked how he will have it done, all he can say is: "Quickly, please, and with a sharp knife." Do not believe that any composers have ever liked it. "None please me," said Selden, after thinking by which of many modes it were best to terminate one's life; and "None please me" is what Rossini, Meyerbeer, Wagner, must often have said to themselves, if they ever considered which of many abridged editions of *Guillaume Tell*, of *Les Huguenots*, of *Lohengrin*, was the least intolerable.

However, if composers choose to write operas which last something like five hours in representation, they must expect to be operated upon; and we may be sure that the light and learned hand of Sir Michael Costa has not been laid upon Herr Wagner in any spirit of cruelty. It seems a pity that he should have cut out the third march; because, although the frequent introduction of

marches may be and doubtless is a weak point with
Herr Wagner, it is a characteristic point, and as such
should have been respected. Some composers at every
opportunity drag in a ballad. Others willingly find
pretext for ballet music. Herr Wagner, in *Lohengrin*,
never misses an occasion for a march. This march madness seizes him first when Elsa is betrothed, secondly
when Elsa is married, thirdly when Lohengrin appears
before the king, the four counts, and the five horses, to
explain who and what he is. Perhaps Herr Wagner takes
refuge in these marches, which the public on their part
welcome as a relief after much unmelodious recitative.
There is nothing dramatically inconsistent in presenting
as a march something that can be marched to; and in
this device the composer, without offending against his
own canons, finds an opportunity of offering from
time to time a piece of rhythmical and well-balanced
music. There is really nothing to complain of in these
marches. They do not help on the action of the drama.
It is obvious, indeed, that they can only retard it;
for scarcely one of the three marches forms an essential part of the piece, as the procession and march in
Le Prophète forms an essential part of that work.
But the *Lohengrin* marches are tuneful, and for that
reason many must welcome them—regretting, indeed,
that instead of only three marches there are not six,
but convinced all the same that not more than one of
the three marches in *Lohengrin* has its place in the

drama where these compositions play, one after the other, the part of the ballad in English opera or of the "legend" in the French opéra comique.

"That reminds me of the legend," says one of the singing personages, probably the prima donna, in almost every example of that peculiar form of the musical drama which, under the name of "opéra comique," prevails in France. "What legend?" says an inquisitive attendant. "The legend of the woman in the red cloak," or perhaps of "The man with the bad hat," replies the leading vocalist. A ritornello is heard in the orchestra, and the legend of the "Man with the bad hat" is introduced. There is something artificial in the process; but it is quite as natural as the perpetual presentation of marching in *Lohengrin*.

One cannot help regretting, in all sincerity, not for the sake of Herr Wagner, who may be presumed to know his own intentions, but for one's own sake and for the sake of the English public, that *Lohengrin*, which contains many points of beauty, should be so terribly long. Elsa's prayer, Lohengrin's entry, the bridal march of the second act, the marriage march of the third act, the duet in the third act for Lohengrin and Elsa, and finally, Lohengrin's declaration, are bright passages in the opera (and many more might be indicated) which everyone must like, and which everyone, as a matter of fact, applauds. The legend which forms the groundwork of the opera is very interesting, the drama is most effectively set forth, the two chief personages are highly poetical figures. Everything, indeed, in *Lohengrin* is admirable except its musical substance, which, apart from the marches of the bridal and wedding scene, and from the fine strains given in many places to the romantic Elsa and to the knightly Lohengrin, is often very nearly intolerable.

Herr Wagner's operas, we are often told, are works which do not depend for their effect on the finished vocalisation nor on the general attractiveness of the prima donna. That much admired personage may find sufficient field for the display of her agreeable talents in operas of the Italian school. For Elsa and Elizabeth some other and higher qualifications are required than those possessed by the " light sopranos " of the ordinary operatic stage; and full of that belief Herr Wagner himself seems to have arrived at the conclusion that neither *Tannhäuser* nor *Lohengrin* would have much chance in an Italian dress. He is known to have told the Queen when he was received by Her Majesty in the course of his first visit to England, now some five-and-twenty years ago, that his operas would not bear translation into Italian. Herr Wagner did not know at the time the resources and capabilities of his own works. He had reckoned, too, without the poetical genius of such artists as Nilsson and Albani; or he never would have said that *Lohengrin* or *Tannhäuser* or the *Flying Dutchman* could not be adequately rendered at an Italian opera-house. Herr Wagner would deserve to be considered a great artistic creator if he had done nothing but give life, form, and character to the three heroines—all of so elevated yet of such a thoroughly human type—known as Senta, Elizabeth, and Elsa. Whether intentionally or instinctively and without any fixed design, he has in each of the three operas known to the English public concentrated nearly all the beauty of the work in the principal female character. But *Tannhäuser* is, above all, worth seeing for Mdlle. Albani's impersonation of Elizabeth, the Christian virgin, saint, and, one may almost add, martyr.

CHAPTER XXIII.

ROBERT THE DEVIL.

ACCORDING to Herr Wagner and his disciples, *Robert le Diable* is the type of all that is ludicrous and monstrous in opera as cultivated by the " Philistines." As a drama *Robert le Diable* is, indeed, not to be compared with *Tannhäuser*.

Apart from a certain want of unity, the personages have neither the reality nor the poetry which belongs to those of *Tannhäuser*; nor does the dramatic action spring, as in *Tannhäuser*, from the natural development of character. One scene after another is presented chiefly for the sake of theatrical effect; and of the long series of scenes many, it must be admitted, are effective. But there is a sad want of poetical

significance in the work as a whole; and that in spite of
the not very exciting victory of good as personified by
Alice over evil as personified by Bertram in the final
scene. Scribe had a good subject to deal with—a subject probably suggested to him by Meyerbeer, who
impressed by the romantic beauty of *Der Freischütz*,
desired, after several moderately successful experiments
with opera in the Italian style, to present in dramatic
music some legendary semi-supernatural theme such as
his former fellow-student, Weber, might have treated.
Scribe, however, was to the librettist of *Der Freischütz*
what the necromancer's servant is in many a tradition to
the necromancer himself. The necromancer pronounces
a formula which works wonders. His servant repeats
the words of the formula; but there is something wanting in his manner of uttering them, and the charm being
imperfect produces no effect. The " Robert the Devil "
legend is intrinsically inferior to the legends of " Don
Juan," " Faust," " Der Freischütz," and " Tannhäuser,"
with all of which it has points in common. But it admitted of better treatment than it has received at the
hands of Scribe; who, while employing all sorts of good
legendary materials in his opera, has failed to give them
consistency. Like the Frenchman's plum-pudding, in
which the constituent elements were all present, not in
pudding-shape, but at the bottom of the saucepan in a
state of solution, so Scribe's *Robert le Diable* is made up
of all that should be included in the composition of a

16 *

good mediæval legend, but without possessing the
legendary physiognomy, form, or flavour. Robert the
Devil is commonly supposed to have been the father of
William the Conqueror. But the learned disagree on
this as on so many other points; and three distinct
theories are entertained as to who " Robert called the
Devil" really was. In the old Norman legend, on the
subject of which an English translation was published
by Wynkyn de Worde in the first years of the sixteenth
century, the malicious *trouvère* to whom the narrative
seems to have been due laid the foundation of endless
disputations by giving no date to the marvellous incidents which he records.

Some, then, say that " Robert called the Devil " was
the Robert, Duke of Normandy, of whom William
the Conqueror was the son; others that he was the
Robert, Duke of Normandy, of whom William the
Conqueror was the father, the holders of this latter
view maintaining that Robert was styled " Devil," and
that his actions were represented as entitling him to
that appellation, in order to please his brother Henry
when Robert had fallen into his power and was
languishing in prison. Robert, however, did not owe
his uncomplimentary surname to his deeds alone, but
rather to the circumstance that his mother, enraged at
having no children, had promised him before his birth to
the fiend. This stamps him as an eldest son, but does
not identify him with the Robert who died in England

any more than with the Robert who lived and died in Normandy.

There was, however, a much earlier Robert celebrated by German chroniclers, who was also given to the devil before his birth, and simply on the condition that he should be born : a Robert who, attended and supported by his familiar spirit, took magic flights in the air, even as Faust afterwards flew supported by the cloak of Mephistopheles. This Robert lived before the settlement of the Normans in France, but was an inhabitant of the country to which the name of Normandy was afterwards to be given. Naturally, then, he was not called "Robert of Normandy," but simply "Robert the Devil." Finding out (through the kindness of friends) what a bad man he was, he went to Rome to see the Pope on the subject, and, more fortunate than Tannhäuser, obtained absolution. He distinguished himself in tournaments, was somehow related to Charlemagne, and, like the Robert le Diable of Scribe, ended by marrying a princess. The legend of this first Robert was possibly applied, with new details, to one or both of those Roberts Dukes of Normandy with whom it is now connected. But there is nothing in the Norman legend of the thirteenth century to show that the Robert whose actions it celebrates was not supposed to have lived several centuries earlier; that he was not, in fact, the Robert of the German chroniclers. Indeed, as will be seen from the next

chapter, Robert is distinctly spoken of in the *trou-
rère's* narrative as a contemporary of Charlemagne.

Robert, then, according to both the German and the
Norman tradition, was in a sense the devil's son; and
Scribe was no doubt thinking of this when in his opera
he made the semi-diabolical Bertram Robert's father.
The author of the traditional poem on the subject in
Norman French makes the young Robert such a bad
boy that he kills his schoolmaster. After that there is
no hope for him until after a long course of evil-doing
he goes to Rome, where he is ordered, by way of
penance, not to speak for a certain number of years,
during which time he travels about with a dog, goes to
the Court of the Emperor, and amuses his Imperial
Majesty by playing practical jokes, of which all that
need be said is that they are worthy of a man who in
his infancy had killed his schoolmaster. Scribe (apart
from the practical jokes) could have done nothing with
a dumb tenor. He had introduced to the public a
dumb prima donna in *La Muette de Portici;* but in that
case he had at least converted the representative of his
principal female character into a *première danseuse.*
Robert could not have been treated in any such manner. His was to be a great singing part; and the only
dumb personage in *Robert le Diable* is the Abbess who,
with her *pas de fascination,* is to Robert what Venus
is to Tannhäuser and Helen to Faust. The Princess
Isabelle has no symbolic part to play. It is the

fascinating abbess, Helena, who tempts Robert ; it is the simple, pure-minded Alice who saves him. Alice is still more directly opposed to Bertram. But Isabelle has nothing to do—or at least nothing that Alice could not do far better. Nor is she, like Alice, Bertram, and Helena, the impersonation of a principle. There are scenes which are significant, such as the gambling scene of the first act, the evocation of the nuns, and the scene in which Alice seeks protection from Bertram by clinging to the cross. But there are also scenes which are unmeaning; and all Robert's proceedings with the magic branch are of this order, unless, indeed, the ingenious librettist desired in presenting them to recall the practical jokes in which the legendary Robert indulged at the Court of the Emperor.

According to Dr. Véron, who, in his " Mémoires d'un Bourgeois de Paris," has given a number of interesting details respecting the first production of *Robert* at the " Académie," of which he was at that time director, the scenery of the third act was so magnificent that Meyerbeer felt positively hurt, and said to the worthy doctor : " You don't think very highly of my music, or you would not pay so much attention to the *mise en scène*. To complete the story, it has been added that in regard to one of the other acts, finding the decorations rather poor, the composer put the proposition quite differently, saying that if the scenery was not good the manager doubtless thought it was all the music merited. *Robert le Diable* demands not only execution of the first order for the musical and dramatic parts of the works, but also excellent dancing, magnificent scenery, brilliant costumes, and every accessory with which an opera can be furnished, including some very elaborate mechanical devices. Other works of incomparably less merit have been played much oftener; for as regards *Robert* the difficulty is to play it at all. Probably it has never been represented quite in accordance with the composer's intentions, except at the Académie of Paris, and not often even there after the dispersion of the original cast, with Nourrit in the part of Robert, Levasseur as Bertram, Mdlle Dorus as Alice, Madame Damoreau as the Princess Isabelle, and Madame Taglioni as the Abbess. But it is a masterpiece on which complete execution is not thrown away; and if it is seldom played to perfection except at the Académie, it must be remembered that at that theatre alone it has been now performed considerably more than five hundred times.

Robert le Diable is, by the way, celebrated for the number of casualties connected with its performance. There is something, perhaps, in the name which brings bad luck as well as good—for, as a rule, operas and theatrical pieces in which diabolical agency is employed are sure to be successful. At all events, when the opera was brought out, no less than three of the principal characters — Alice, who represents the good

principle; Bertram, who is the evil principle incarnate;
and Robert himself, who is something between the two
—had only a very narrow escape of serious injuries.
As Alice made her entry in the third act a board
bearing a dozen lighted lamps fell with a crash on
the stage, just at Mdlle. Dorus's feet. Soon afterwards, in the same act, a very solid cloud was just
falling on the recumbent figure of the Abbess when
Mdlle. Taglioni saw what was coming, and, with an
agility which was never more serviceable to her than
then, rose from her tomb and escaped before the
dangerous mass had actually descended. An incident
still more ominous in appearance, though nothing very
dreadful resulted from it, happened in the last act,
at the very conclusion of the opera. At the close
of the trio Bertram had to disappear through a trap;
and no sooner had he done so than Robert, to the
horror of the public who had somehow managed to
arrive at a comprehension of the story, followed him.
No preparations had been made for the hero's reception below; and for a minute or so it was the general
impression that he had really come to a bad end.
But Nourrit, his representative, appeared on the stage
to show that he was still alive; and the audience then
probably thought that they had only been witnessing,
without quite understanding it, one more of those pantomime tricks in which this magnificent work abounds.

With all due deference to existing prejudices, it may

be maintained that the part of Alice is not a part for the "robust" soprano at all, still less for a soprano of such remarkable robustness as belongs to some of its more recent impersonators. The distinction between "light soprano" and "dramatic soprano" had scarcely been invented forty years ago when *Robert le Diable* was first produced. A soprano of the first rank was supposed to be capable of singing all kinds of soprano music. Pasta was quite equal to the execution of the lightest of what are called "light" parts; and Malibran would have been much astonished if she had been told that, because she was admirable as Rosina in *Il Barbiere* and as Norina in *L'Elisir*, it was therefore out of the question for her to attempt such characters as Semiramide and Desdemona. *Les Huguenots* seems to have been the first opera in which, parts being provided for two sopranos, one was furnished with airs of a florid and purely ornamental character, the other with expressive airs of real dramatic significance; and gradually it has become an accepted rule that Valentine in *Les Huguenots* and Alice in *Robert le Diable* belong to the category of "strong dramatic" parts, while the character of Marguerite in the former and that of Isabelle in the latter are regarded as equally adapted to the "light soprano" voice. The fact, however, is that the music given to the Princess Isabelle is much more dramatic in the true sense of the word (witness the scene with Robert, in which Isabelle's grand air occurs) than that assigned to Alice. If the question of personal appearance be considered, the Princess might well have a more majestic bearing than the peasant girl. But in composing *Robert le Diable*, neither the librettist nor the author of the music was thinking of any contrast between the voices and vocalisation of the two principal female characters. In accordance with the well-known distinction observed in so many French dramas and comedies, the part of Isabelle was conceived as something in the line of the " grande coquette " (who is not necessarily a " coquette " any more than an " opéra comique" is necessarily a " comic opera "); while that of Alice was simply a part for the " ingénue." Mdme. Patti could play it, as she plays everything, to perfection; Mdlle. Albani, too, would be a charming Alice; and Mdme. Nilsson, who has already appeared in the character, is probably the best Alice yet seen. But some of the stouter representatives of the character are no more fitted for the part than for that of Gilda in *Rigoletto*.

Robert le Diable has, as already remarked, been pointed to as a typical specimen of the "grand opera," with such merits as may belong to it and with all its faults. It is, indeed, a very favourable example of lyric drama as treated by a great master under the very precise conditions laid down by the traditions and rules of the so-called " Académie." The true defect of the *Robert le Diable* consists in the fact that the subject is not poetically treated—as, for instance, *Lohengrin*, *Tannhäuser*, and the *Flying Dutchman* have been treated by Wagner. Scribe believed in the legend of Robert the Devil about as much as a pastrycook believes in flour, butter, and sugar; enough, that is to say, for his immediate purposes as an operatic confectioner. Wagner, if he had adopted the legend of Robert the Devil at all, would have inspired himself with its full meaning, and would have imagined a work which, however full of symbols and wonders, would have been consistent though impossible, and truthful though unreal. Nevertheless, as operas go, *Robert le Diable* may fairly be considered a masterpiece. It presents a number of well-marked musical personages, contains a good many highly dramatic scenes, and is as full of melodies as an opera well can be. It is the one grand opera, moreover, of the Académie pattern, in which the ballet and ballet-dancers are not dragged in, so to say, by the head and shoulders. The dancing divertisse-ment forms part and parcel of the opera; the principal ballerina being one of the leading characters in the work.

CHAPTER XXIV.

MEYERBEER SINCE ROBERT LE DIABLE.

OF the series of great works composed by Meyerbeer for the Paris Opera House which, beginning with *Robert le Diable* (1831), ended with *L'Africaine* (1865), the one which has met with the greatest success in London is decidedly *Les Huguenots.* Of that success, however, much has been due to the fact that for a number of years the parts of Raoul and of Valentine were taken at the Royal Italian Opera by Signor Mario and Mdme. Grisi; at Her Majesty's Theatre by Signor Giuglini and Mdlle. Titiens. Of these four great artists three are no more; while the last survivor of the quartet, or rather of the double duet, has left the operatic stage, and now holds the post of Conservator at one of the public museums of Rome. The only artist of the first merit that the London public has now the opportunity of hearing in *Les Huguenots* is Mdme. Trebelli; and it would be impossible to speak too highly of Mdme. Trebelli's Urbano, an impersonation as remarkable for its brilliancy as for its charm. Urbano's part is no insignificant element in the concerted music of the opening act. But Urbano's airs are the two most genuine melodies in the opera. In adding a second solo to the part Meyerbeer doubled the importance of the character. The second air is known to have been composed for Mdme. Alboni; but it might have been written expressly for Mdme. Trebelli, so perfectly is it suited to this artist's graceful and expressive style.

It is now upwards of thirty years since *Le Prophète* was first performed at the Royal Italian Opera, with a cast which included Mario as John of Leyden, Mdme. Viardot as Fidès, Miss Catherine Hayes as Bertha, and Tagliafico as the Count of Oberthal. Of these artists only one is still engaged at Covent Garden; and Signor Tagliafico, the senior member of Mr. Gye's company, is no longer heard as a singer, but confines the exercise of his remarkable artistic talent to the general superintendence of operatic "business" on the stage. Besides Signor Mario, Signor Tamberlik, and M. Roger, the creator of the part at the Paris Opera House, have been heard at Covent Garden as John of Leyden. Mdme. Viardot, too, had successors in the character of

Fidès among whom Mdme. Csillag and Mdme. Titiens may be mentioned; for, during one brief season, Mr. Gye and Mr. Mapleson combined their forces, and under their joint management *Le Prophète* was brought out with Mdlle. Titiens and Signor Mongini in the two principal parts.

Of the tenors now before the public, not one has enough physical strength for such a part as that of John of Leyden, of which one at least of the airs—the famous hymn at the end of the third act, accompanied by much brass in the orchestra, by a chorus of enthusiasts on the stage, and by the rising sun at the back of the stage—might have been written more appropriately for a trumpet than for the human voice. The " pastorale," again, sung by John of Leyden while he is still in his peaceful mood is very trying to all tenors whose upper notes are not in the most perfect condition.

The difficulties the representative of Fidès has to contend with are quite of another kind. The character makes great demands on its representative's histrionic powers. It must be played with high intelligence and here and there with much subtlety of expression. The two leading personages stand out so prominently from the rest of the characters that, with a really able John of Leyden and an equally able Fidès, the opera at a generally well-appointed establishment can scarcely fail to be effective. Real ability, however, in these

exacting parts is only possible to artists of genius.
For a fit impersonation of the hero the voice and
talent of a Mario, for the fit impersonation of the
hero's mother the talent and voice of a Viardot, are
wanted.

Le Prophète, the third of the series of great works
written by Meyerbeer for the Paris Opera House,
demands a more perfect execution than any of the
others. There is very little human interest in the
opera, which may almost be said to depend for its
success on the music alone. Some suspicious son of
the Church discovered soon after the production of *Le
Prophète* that Meyerbeer's object in composing the
sort of trilogy formed by *Le Prophète, Les Huguenots,*
and *Robert le Diable,* was to bring religion of all kinds,
or at least the principal forms of Christianity, into
contempt. In Robert we have a striking picture of
the profligacy of nuns; the plot of *Les Huguenots* is
based on the sanguinary contests between Catholics
and Protestants; *Le Prophète* exhibits the fanaticism
of a Protestant sect, and the fanaticism combined with
sensuality of the conscious impostor who has founded
it. Oddly enough, Meyerbeer was to make one more
attack upon religious fanaticism in the last of his
operas, *L'Africaine;* which brings out forcibly in one
of its principal scenes the bigotry and stupidity of the
Inquisition. But, apart from all question of religion
and morality, *Le Prophète* has the disadvantage of

being uninteresting in an ordinary dramatic point of view. The subject is borrowed partly from the history of John of Leyden, partly, and indeed principally, from that of the false Demetrius, who, when he had raised himself to the throne of Russia, was confronted with his humbly-born mother, even as John of Leyden, the tailor (or, as M. Scribe has preferred to represent him, innkeeper), is confronted in the coronation scene with the unhappy Fidès. In the first act Fidès has just arrived from a journey in search of Bertha, a young girl betrothed to her son. But the powerful and wicked lord of the manor, Count Oberthal, forbids the banns, and, to render the projected marriage impossible, seizes the fair Bertha and her would-be mother-in-law and imprisons them both in his castle. Three Anabaptists—terrible personages who for the last thirty years have been allowed the privilege by a licence which has now become a tradition to sing out of tune—profit by this example of aristocratic tyranny to raise the inhabitants of the surrounding districts against their proprietors and feudal lords.

When John of Leyden is introduced we find that this future fanatic is at present nothing more than an amiable visionary, who dreams that he is called upon to save the nations and will one day be their king. This "illumined" personage is just such an instrument as the Anabaptists are in search of. But he wishes to bring peace, not war, to suffering humanity; and

nothing can be made of him until, happily for the
designs of the religious insurgents, his mother and his
betrothed appear before him pursued by the troops
of the ferocious Count. To save his mother from
the blows of the brutal soldiery he surrenders to
them his bride. But he is now determined upon
revenge, and without further hesitation joins the
Anabaptists.

These incidents occupy the first two acts. The third
act represents the camp of the Anabaptists in West-
phalia. John has defeated the troops sent against him,
and he seems disposed to resign his command, when
Count Oberthal, who has become his prisoner, informs
him that Bertha has thrown herself into the river, and,
swimming across it, has taken refuge at Münster.
John now no longer thinks of laying down his sword.
Münster must be besieged; and in the fourth act we
find ourselves inside the town, where Bertha is seen
disguised as a pilgrim, while the aged Fidés is wandering about the place begging her bread. Bertha, on
the strength of a rumour, believes that John is dead,
and, filled with rage against the so-called Prophet,
whom she regards as the true author of the war in which
her lover has perished, resolves on the first opportunity
to stab the monster. In the second scene of this act—
one of the most magnificent in the whole range of
spectacular opera—John, at once Prophet and King, is
crowned in the cathedral. His followers and the people

generally regard him as an emissary from heaven, when suddenly he is recognised by his poor old mother. John tries to magnetise her by his saintly and imperial look; and if in this brief dumb scene between Fidès and her son the gestures and demeanour of the performers do not entirely absorb the attention of the spectator, some heed should be given to the eloquent and touching phrases by which the supposed emotions of the semi-divine Prophet and his very human mother are expressed in the orchestra. Fidès recognises John, is disavowed by him, and at last, in ambiguous language, acknowledges her error, exclaiming that she "no longer has a son."

Le Prophète is worth seeing for the coronation scene alone. The well-known march, one of Meyerbeer's most famous instrumental pieces; the religious choruses, accompanied alternately by the organ and by the orchestra, or by the organ and orchestra combined; the highly ecclesiastical, purely melodic phrase sung in unison by the choir of officiating boys in their cardinal-like vestments of red—all the details of this musical picture, so complete and so impressive as a whole, are perfectly brought out. The finale to this, the grandest of many grand scenes conceived and realised by Meyerbeer, contains one very original feature. A passionate solo, already sung by Fidès as the expression of her despair, is repeated in

17 *

fragments, alternately with fragments of the coronation service; the interest of the audience being thus
divided between the triumph of the false Prophet
and the despondent condition of his true-hearted
mother.

The last act is shorter than the preceding ones.
The historical John of Leyden was made prisoner
and executed; but a much more brilliant end is reserved for the John of Leyden of Scribe and Meyerbeer's opera.   After an interview with his mother,
whose pardon he implores in a prison where he has
thought it prudent to confine her, this Dutch Sardanapalus blows himself up in the midst of an orgie
with the dancing girls and female attendants of various
descriptions who are taking part in his little celebration.   For one moment he had thought of flying with
his mother and the innocent Bertha, who visits the
unhappy Fidès in her prison.   But Bertha, though a
simple village girl, is of more heroic cast than the
sham hero who has been playing the part of the Prophet.   Her first object is now to *écraser l'infâme* in
the shape of the half superstitious and half sensual
monster who has caused so much misery.   This she
proposes to accomplish by setting fire to a mine which,
she has somehow ascertained, will, on being exploded,
lay his palace in ruins and crush him beneath them.
Finding, however, that the Prophet and her lover are

one and the same man, and meeting the impostor face to face in the prison, she puts an end to her own life. In the final scene the Prophet comes down from his throne to sing a drinking song of a very impulsive character, and which to be effective should be sung with great energy. The intervals of the solo are filled by a graceful chorus of female voices with harp accompaniments. At last an explosion is heard, and in the midst of the flames everything falls to pieces. With the Prophet himself die not only those who had administered to his pleasures, but also a large number of his enemies, who have surrounded the palace and been admitted within its precincts sufficiently to have an opportunity of taking part in the catastrophe. There is something grand in this final scene, of which the idea does not, of course, belong to M. Scribe. But Scribe and Meyerbeer have shown how admirably the end of Sardanapalus might be treated in operatic fashion. It may even be said that in opera alone could such a scene—with the dancing and singing and the sound of all kinds of musical instruments which should accompany it—be rendered with due effect.

Besides the final scene of the orgie and the incomparable coronation scene, one of the features in *Le Prophète* is the highly picturesque skating scene of the second act.

L'Africaine may be fairly described as a geographical

opera, and if it was in need of a second title, none more appropriate than *Le Cap des Tempétes* could be suggested. Oddly enough, the title as it now stands involves a geographical, or rather, one should say, an ethnological, error. The so-called Africaine does not come from any part of Africa, but from the Island of Madagascar in the Indian Ocean. As Vasco di Gama remarks himself—" Sous le soleil d'Afrique elle n'a pas pris naissance." Why, then, call her L'Africaine ?

The opera commences quietly enough with a romance " Adieu, rive du Tage," for Ines, one of the ladies of the Portuguese Court, whose part is somewhat analogous to that of Bertha in *Le Prophète*. Ines is the fair heroine, the light soprano heroine, the heroine with roulades—contrasting with Selika (L'Africaine) the dark passionate dramatic heroine. A tenor with anything like a part must have at least two women in love with him; and Vasco di Gama has gained the heart both of Selika and of Ines. Selika on her side is beloved only by Nelusko, a fellow-countryman of hers, who with herself has been purchased at an African slave-market by Vasco di Gama. Thus while Nelusko loves Selika, Selika loves Vasco di Gama, who thinks only of Ines, who is obliged by her father to think of Don Pedro, President of the King's Council.

Ines's opening romance possesses a certain dramatic

importance from the fact that she will have to repeat a few bars of it behind the scenes at the end of the fourth act, when Vasco believes her to be no longer in existence. When the Duke of Mantua in *Rigoletto*, after he is thought to have been assassinated, makes known his presence to the world by singing "La donna e mobile," the audience cannot forget the striking melody that they have heard over and over again only a few minutes before. Ines's romance is undeniably graceful; it may be objected to it, however, that it is not tuneful enough to be generally remembered when it is introduced at the end of the fourth act for the especial purpose of being recognised as belonging to Ines.

Ines has been told that Vasco di Gama has perished in a shipwreck, and in a short time is urged by her father to accept the hand of Don Pedro, when suddenly Vasco di Gama enters. He alone of a large crew has been saved, and he now comes to tell the Grand Assembly of councillors and inquisitors that having passed the Cape of Good Hope he has discovered a strange land. Let them grant him a ship and he will seize the territory in the name of the King of Portugal. The ecclesiastical members of the council reply in the style of the famous encyclical letter, and refuse to admit the existence of a country hitherto unknown to the Church. Vasco di Gama quotes against the inquisitors the well-known case of Christopher Columbus.

But they will not listen to his arguments. He then insults them, and as a punishment for his irreverence is condemned to perpetual imprisonment.

In this long and elaborate finale, constituting the greater portion of the first act, Vasco di Gama has some fine declamatory passages, which a capable tenor can always deliver with good effect. The "chorus of bishops" is very imposing, and the whole scene is as grand and as full of movement as the scene of the "blessings of the daggers" in the *Huguenots*, to which, as regards construction, it bears a striking resemblance. The worst of it is that all this grand music rests upon a very insufficient dramatic foundation. In the *Huguenots* the musical tempest swells, not without cause. In *L'Africaine* the inquisitors repeat a magnificent phrase, louder and louder, until at last, declaimed by all the voices on the stage, and supported by the force of the orchestra, it fills the theatre with sound—and what, after all, is it about? Still the encyclical letter and the denunciation of Vasco di Gama's project for passing the Cape as one of the errors of modern liberalism !

In the second act we find Vasco di Gama with his two slaves, Selika and Nelusko, in prison. Vasco is asleep. Selika watches over him and sings him one of the songs of her native Madagascar,—a wild passionate air. This "Chant du Sommeil" is followed by a characteristic and highly dramatic song, in which Nelusko's love for Selika and his detestation of Vasco di Gama are expressed alternately and in admirable contrast. Nelusko is *the* character of the opera, and Meyerbeer has put his mark upon him, as upon Bertram in *Robert le Diable*, on Marcel in *Les Huguenots*, and (in quite a different style) on the timid superstitious peasant in *Dinorah*. After Nelusko's air Selika wakes Vasco di Gama and gives him a lesson in geography. A map of the African coast from the Straits of Gibraltar to the Cape of Good Hope hangs conveniently on the prison wall, and Vasco, looking at it, exclaims :—

"Ill-omened Cape, what toil and trouble
Are lost in seeking thee to double " ; *
"Steer to the left you die " (replies Selika) ; "steer to the right,
A large and lovely isle comes to the sight."
"Heavens ! I see it all ! " (cries Vasco), "O fatal Cape,
Thy perils now the sailor may escape."

The grateful pupil then takes his mistress in his arms, calls her an angel and embraces her. Poor Selika imagines that Vasco loves her for her own sake. Ines, who enters the prison at the very height of Vasco's geographical ardour, falls into the same error. She has come to tell him that he is free, and she has

* Terrible et fatal promontoire
Que nul n'apu doubler encore.

purchased his freedom by giving her hand to Don Pedro, the President of the Council. Scandal had asserted that Selika was not Vasco's mistress in geography alone; and Ines had believed the calumny. To prove that it has no foundation, the noble-hearted Vasco offers Selika to Ines as a present; and both Selika and Nelusko enter the household of Don Pedro and his young wife. It then appears that the Council of State have granted to Don Pedro what they refused to Vasco, and have placed him in command of a naval expedition, at the head of which he proposes to "double the Cape." Hearing this and discovering that Don Pedro has at the same time deprived him of his project and his bride, Vasco bursts into a fit of indignation, and reproaches Ines for her inconstancy; Selika reproaches Vasco for his ingratitude; Ines is in despair; Don Pedro exults over the misfortunes of his rival; while Nelusko flatters himself with the hope that he will one day be able to make Don Pedro as unhappy as Vasco has been made already.

In the third act we are introduced to the celebrated ship, which occupies the whole of the stage, and, indeed, *is* the stage. It is motionless and has the appearance of a fixture; but that, of course, is because the sea is calm. Its upper and lower decks, on which the sailors sing hymns, the cabins, in which the women talk, sing, and say their prayers—in short, the whole of the "inner life" of a Portuguese man-of-war—may be seen. The ship, or section of a ship, looks very much like a house of which the front has been pulled down. There is appropriate music for each story, and those who remember the finale to the second act of *L'Etoile du Nord* understand how effectively Meyerbeer has combined the songs of the women with those of the sailors. The double chorus of sailors, " O grand Saint Dominique," is a magnificent composition, well worthy the attention of our choral societies. After the concerted chorus comes a very original and fantastic ballad for Nelusko, which, without bearing any resemblance in detail to the " pifpaff " song in the *Huguenots*, is, nevertheless, written in much the same style. The subject of the ballad is the legend of Adamastor, " the giant of the storm," and it contains an ironical warning to the Portuguese sailors, who little suspect that a tempest is about to break out, and that, thanks to Nelusko's guidance, the ship will be dashed to pieces on the rocks. Suddenly Vasco, who has been doubling the Cape on his own account, makes his appearance on Don Pedro's vessel, and urges him to place no confidence in Nelusko, who is steering to certain destruction. After a violent altercation between Vasco and Don Pedro, which is made the groundwork of a not very remarkable duet, Vasco is sentenced to be shot for mutinous conduct, and the order is about to be carried out when the ship strikes somewhere on the coast of Madagascar.

The stage now begins to rock, the orchestra growls and roars, the sailors swear, the women shriek, and we understand that the vessel is being wrecked. At the same time a number of Malays rush on board, and run a muck through the unfortunate Europeans. Vasco is saved by the powerful influence of Selika, who a slave in Portugal is in Madagascar a queen. This, however, we do not know until the fourth act, when it appears that all the crew of the Portuguese vessel have been sacrificed. The men have been put to the sword, the women have been taken by the half-civilised Nelusko to die in a quiet lady-like manner beneath the upas-tree. The fourth act opens with a chorus of natives, followed by an " Indian march " of the most gorgeous character. In the beautiful air, " O paradis sorti de l'onde," Vasco expresses the delight with which the mere fact of being in Madagascar inspires him. He seems very happy, aad having no female acquaintance in the island except Selika, makes love to her, on the principle, no doubt, that " Quand on n'a pas ce qu'on aime, if faut aimer ce qu'on a." The duet in which Selika and Vasco interchange vows is the finest piece in the opera. If the finale to the first act may be compared to the blessing of the daggers in the *Huguenots,* if the combined choruses of the third act recall the finale to the second act of *L'Etoile du Nord,* if Nelusko's fantastic ballad is in the style of the " pif-paff " song in the *Huguenots,* then the grand duet between Selika and Vasco can only be likened to the grand duet in the *Huguenots* between Valentine and Raoul.

Unfortunately, it is impossible to feel any sympathy for Vasco, who deserves to be told, as Rousseau was told by a certain young lady at Venice, to "leave women and study mathematics." Having first bought Selika, he has afterwards studied mathematics and navigation at her feet, always pretending to entertain great affection for her. Then, to show that he does not care for her in the least, he brutally gives her away, or sells her (it is not clear which) to the fair Ines. Now, having no other woman near him, he affects once more to love her; but no sooner has he married her according to the laws and customs of Madagascar, than, Ines coming to life again, he resolves to desert her for the sake of Don Pedro's widow. However, Meyerbeer has given him very beautiful music to sing, and listening to the music, we forget the man's morals, which are really worse than those of Don Juan. Don Juan does not pretend to be much better than he is—at least, not in Mozart's opera. But Vasco di Gama is perpetually talking of immortality, glory, and of the immense good he is doing to his fellow-creatures. The chief excuse to be made for him in the matter of his marriage with Selika is that he must pass as her husband or die. Selika, too, prepares him for the ceremony by plying him freely with intoxicating drink, of which she herself

partakes.   If in these particulars M. Scribe has given
a faithful picture of royal manners in Madagascar, one
can understand the introduction of the article in the
last Madagascar Constitution, by which the queen is
forbidden to touch strong liquor.

The admirable love-duet between Vasco and Selika
is followed by a dance and chorus of Selika's female
attendants, of which the pure simple melody is enchant-
ing.   A few moments before the fall of the curtain, the
voice of Ines is heard singing the romance of the first
act, " Adieu, rive du Tage."   Vasco, who is now very
far gone, exclaims that the voice must come from
heaven.   He hesitates, however, about following Selika,
upon which he is surrounded by bayaderes who, singing
and dancing, carry him off to the palace of their queen.

The fifth act, unlike fifth acts in general, is highly
dramatic, and it has also the advantage of being short.
It contains two remarkable vocal pieces—a duet for Ines
and Selika, and the air sung by Selika as she goes to
sleep and sleeping dies beneath the upas-tree.   The
duet occurs in an effective situation, and is the most
dramatic duet for female voices that Meyerbeer has
written.   At the end of the duet Selika, instead of
taking vengeance on her rival, resolves to sacrifice herself.   She sends Ines and Vasco to the coast, where
Vasco's ship still remains, and prepares to die.   The
scene changes and shows us a promontory overlooking
the sea.   In the middle of the stage, erect, with wide-

spreading branches, stands the fatal *mancenillier*, admirably represented, as, indeed, is all the tropical scenery of this part of the drama.   Selika walks towards the sea—"immense et sans limite, ainsi que ma douleur"—and looks at it in silence.   The orchestra in the meanwhile gives expression to her grief in a ritornello, which soon became celebrated and which is the most moving strain in the opera.   It is curious to notice the effect of this bold, powerful, but eminently simple passage upon the audience, who are as much touched by it as though the sound of the violoncellos, altos, and bassoons, all speaking in unison, . were that of a living voice.   No music could be more eloquent.   But though eloquence must naturally obtain a response, it would be better were the audience not to utter the murmurs of applause which one particular note, or, rather, one particular interval, in this ritornello calls forth, until the whole is at an end.

"What is the ritornello like?" it may be asked. But how can words convey any definite idea of music and, above all, of pure melody.   All one can say is, that it bears the unmistakeable stamp of the composer.   It is of Meyerbeer, Meyerbeerish; and if you hear it once in *L'Africaine*, you will never hear it again without thinking of the black leaves and crimson flowers of the *mancenillier*, and of the sea, "immense and illimitable," like the grief of Selika, whose wild, bitter, unappeasable sorrow it seems to express.

Selika lies down beneath the fatal tree, sings, sees visions, hears voices in the air, proclaiming her union with Vasco, then is awakened to the reality of her position by the sound of a gun fired from his departing ship, and dies, exclaiming : " it was only a dream."

In the final scene of *L'Africaine* Meyerbeer is graceful and tender, as in *Dinorah*, of which we are reminded — partly, perhaps, because the scene of the moonlight upon the water recalls Dinorah's shadow-scene, partly because the gentle Africaine is now in the same dreamy state as that in which we are accustomed to see Dinorah, and principally because Selika's air is in the same time and has much the same character as melodic Dinorah's " Ombre légère."

The scene of the upas-tree, which may be looked upon as the parent, not the outcome, of the four preceding acts, is one of the finest and one of the most perfectly suited for musical illustration in the whole range of the lyric drama. Everyone can understand Meyerbeer's being struck with it, as it was first pointed out to him in an old English melodrama, and thereupon determining to base an opera upon it, or rather to construct an opera, of which the said scene of the forsaken woman dying voluntarily beneath the upas-tree should form the climax ; but no one can understand the full beauty of the scene who has not witnessed its actual performance. Her despair as she looks at the sea, " vast and illimitable as her grief," on which her treacherous lover is about to sail away from her for ever, is agonising; but her closing scene, when, with the voices of consoling spirits in her ears, she lies down and dies, is full of tenderness, and, though infinitely touching, by no means horrible. The drama ends as happily as is possible, inasmuch as for the poor heart-broken Selika life is not possible; and one leaves the theatre full of compassion for the Queen of Madagascar, and with a strong desire to hear Mdme. Lucca again at the earliest opportunity.

There is a Scribe Theatre in some Italian city; there is, or was, a Beaumarchais Theatre in Paris; and the Royal Italian Opera, if it were not already sufficiently well named (for the operas produced there are always sung in the Italian language), might be called the Meyerbeer Theatre. Nowhere in Europe has Meyerbeer's music been so systematically cultivated as at the Royal Italian Opera, except, perhaps, at the Royal Opera of Berlin, where, as at our chief lyrical theatre, both his so-called comic and his justly-named "serious" works are performed. The Royal Italian Opera did not, to be sure, invent Meyerbeer, nor the style in which Meyerbeer's great musical dramas are placed on the stage. But whereas in Paris his *Pardon de Ploermel* and *Etoile du Nord* are to be heard only at the Opéra Comique, and his four grand operas only at the celebrated theatre which, until the last few years, was known by the absurd designation of "Academy," the repertory of Covent Garden includes all his works, or, at least, all those recognised by him as legitimate productions, to the exclusion of his three or four bastard Italian works brought out before the " Robert the Devil " period.

The *Star of the North* may be a masterpiece, but it is certainly not Meyerbeer's masterpiece. It was formed out of material already used in construction of an opera called *The Camp of Silesia,* in which the chief historical character was not Peter the Great, but Frederick the Great, and in which the flute-playing propensities of Mr. Carlyle's hero were turned to good account. It is very remarkable that in those heroic countries Russia and Prussia four sovereigns whom their admiring subjects thought worthy of being styled " Great " were produced in the same half-century: the great Elector and Frederick the Great in the former, and Peter the Great and Catherine the Great in the latter. This was certainly quick work, seeing that in England we have had no " great " sovereign, or, at least, no sovereign formally so called, from the Norman Conquest to the present day.

On the other hand, neither Frederick II. nor Peter I., in spite of their " greatness," have escaped the indignity of being presented to the public as operatic heroes ; a fate they have had to share with innumerable troubadours, muleteers, brigands, and other persons of doubtful character. The Prussian censorship objected, it is true, to "the Great Frederick" being made to figure on the stage as a flute-player; and the drunkenness of Peter was, of course, not thought a fit subject for stage presentation at St. Petersburg.

No superingenious critic has yet pointed out that Meyerbeer, in dwelling so much on Frederick the Great's passion for the flute, and on Peter the Great's habits of intoxication, may have wished to bring kingship into contempt. It has already been observed that in *Robert the Devil* he attacks the conventual system by representing an orgie of resuscitated nuns; that in the *Huguenots* he exhibits religious intolerance, as shown so strikingly in the massacre of St. Bartholomew's Day; that in *Le Prophète* he gives a picture of religious fanaticism and religious imposture: in short, that in his three greatest works he shows himself "the enemy of religion," as in two of his minor works (it might equally be maintained) he shows himself no respecter of monarchy.

The opera in which Peter the Great figures is full of originality, and of a certain sort of character. The stage Peter is not either mentally, morally, or physically—though there are plenty of his portraits extant— a whit like the Peter of history. The Catherine is still less like the historical Catherine, of whose vulgarity and immorality a striking account is given in Mr. Carlyle's "Frederic." Danilowitz the pieman

18 *

may or may not be like the first of the Menschtchi-
koffs for whom he stands, and whose name (but for
a remonstrance from the old prince) he would actually
have borne. As for Gritzenko, one of the most important characters of the opera, he is so thoroughly, so
outrageously Russian, that as a man he unites in himself some of the peculiarities of the inhabitants of every
part of Russia, while as a soldier he seems to belong
to every corps in the Russian army The termination
" enko " proclaims his name to be Little Russian, and
we are not astonished when we hear him styled a
" Cossack." But he is also called a Calmuck, as if a
Calmuck and a Cossack were the same thing. However he is generally described as a Cossack, from which
one would 'naturally take him for a cavalry soldier.
This, however, cannot be, for he takes offence on hearing the Russian cavalry praised, and thereupon begins
singing a song in honour of the Russian infantry; to
which as a Cossack or even as a Calmuck he naturally
would not belong. Somehow or other, too, in spite of
his Little Russian name, and of the designation of Cossack so frequently bestowed upon him (in common
with that of Calmuck), he wears the uniform of the
Pavlovsky regiment of the Imperial Guard, whose
helmets are conic sections. The regiment named in
honour of Paul did not exist in the time of Peter; but
the process of " robbing Peter to pay Paul " has so
long been carried on, that once in a way there can be

no harm in reversing it. Moreover, if the conic-sectional helmets of the Pavlovsky regiment are introduced at all, each helmet should exhibit a bullet-hole; it being a tradition in this remarkable corps to get shot through the head, and, whatever may be done with the arms, never to abandon the helmets, which are transferred from the dead to the living, so that the soldier of to-day wears, or fancies he wears, the identical helmet worn by some soldier in the time of the Emperor Paul. It is a fact, too, as everyone who has ever seen one or more soldiers of the Pavlovsky regiment must be aware, that no man is admitted into it who has not a turn-up nose.

M. Scribe has been often attacked for his ignorance or wilful perversion of history—so often and severely that at last, in his preface to " Les Vêpres Siciliennes," he replied to the charge, and as regards this particular piece, begged his critics not to accuse him of falsifying the story of the Sicilian Vespers, inasmuch as that story, however generally accepted, was fabulous. M. Scribe looked upon history as so much material for making operas, comedies, and vaudevilles out of ; and he cut it, clipped it, and trimmed it until he got it into the shape that suited him. If he met with material of a promising kind he did not ask where it came from, any more than a tailor would ask at what mill and by what particular process an attractive piece of cloth had been manufactured. A personage supposed to be historical was always historical enough for M. Scribe if he was characteristic; so was an incident, if it was dramatic and picturesque. M. Scribe's libretto *à la Russe* is not more improbable nor more incorrect in its details than many other of his libretti; and it has given Meyerbeer the opportunity of writing some admirable dramatic music, including a part—that of Catarina—which, as played by Patti at the Royal Italian Opera, seems the most charming that he has ever created.

If Beaumarchais and Victor Hugo had been contemporaries, they might have disputed as to whether Mdme. Patti's dramatic genius rendered her a fitter representative of comic or of tragic characters; and the number is certainly small of actresses who, like Mdme. Patti, have been equally vivacious in comedy and impressive in the serious drama. Preserving the liveliest recollection of Mdme. Patti's performances as Elvira in *Ernani*, and as Rosina in the *Barber of Seville*, one cannot say whether she is most successful in what are called "dramatic" parts or in those lighter ones which were at one time thought suited, above all others, to her brilliant style. The music of Catarina in the *Etoile du Nord* belongs, equally with that of Catarina in the *Crown Diamonds*, to the domain of the light soprano. Written for Mdme. Caroline Duprez, daughter of the great tenor of the same name, it was first introduced to the public of the Royal Italian Opera by the graceful

Mdme. Bosio, who made of the part one of the most charming of her many charming impersonations. The beautiful melody sung by the departing Catarina at the end of the first act, which, commencing as a prayer, terminates as a barcarolle, gives the singer the oppor-. tunity of distinguishing herself both in the plain and in the florid style; the lively narrative and descriptive couplets which Catarina delivers immediately after her entry are quite of another character, and suggest the Opéra Comique of Paris; while the thoroughly pretty "gipsy rondo" has again a colour of its own, though neither Mr. Borrow nor the Abbé Liszt, nor any other student of gipsy peculiarities, would be able to recognise it as of "romany" origin. Meyerbeer's music is always "characteristic"; but "characteristic of what?" one is obliged now and then to ask.

In the first act of the *Etoile du Nord* we hear a chorus of Russian workmen employed in Finland; and whether the sounds uttered be intended to suggest Finland or Russia they are appropriately uncouth, and give one an idea of a rough, primitive, and somewhat melancholy-minded people. The gipsy rondo presents no art of resemblance to the airs actually sung by those Russian "tsigani" whom Sir Arthur Helps has made the subject of some admirable chapters in his "Ivan de Biron." But the delicate though spirited melody, taking it with the accompanying chorus of bar-barians, makes one think of a fairy surrounded by

goblins or a nightingale among bears; so that the
whole piece, whether specially " characteristic" or not,
is at least highly dramatic.   In the second act the
military music, of which this act mainly consists, is indeed " characteristic " in the fullest sense of the word;
nor was it difficult to give the character of infantry
music to no matter what tune in march time, accompanied by infantry drums; while cavalry music would
naturally be suggested by the employment of such
brass instruments as are specially used in cavalry bands.
The fife-and-drum music, too, tells its own story;
and the march which predominates in the grand concerted finale above the two other airs used in combination with it possesses not only a military but an
historical character.   It belongs, it is true, not to the
Russians but to the Prussians; from whom, however,
Meyerbeer may have supposed the Russians to have
borrowed it, as they borrowed so many things of a
military kind, including those mitre-like helmets worn
by Peter's troops in *L'Etoile du Nord,* which even now
are worn as a matter of tradition by one regiment in
the Russian army, and which in Hogarth's time seem
to have been worn by our own Foot Guards.

The confusion of things Prussian with things Russian
in *L'Etoile du Nord* is to be accounted for by the fact
that what is now the *Star of the North* was formerly, in
part at least, the *Camp of Silesia,* and that in accepting
a Russian in lieu of a Prussian subject the composer has

not always been able to make the substitution perfect
in regard to details. As it has ceased to exist in its
original independent form, nothing need now be said
of the *Camp of Silesia*; except that a large portion of its
materials has been used in the construction of *L'Etoile
du Nord*; that the part of the heroine was written
for Jenny Lind; and that the air with obbligato flute
accompaniment (really a duet for flute and voice),
which is now sung so charmingly and with such admirable effect by Mdme. Adelina Patti in the third act of
L'Etoile du Nord, was formerly sung by the "Swedish
Nightingale" in the Prussian opera on which the Russian opera is based.

As in *Les Diamants de la Couronne, Le Domino
Noir*, and so many other operas, the eminent librettist, has made a point in *L'Etoile du Nord* of exhibiting his heroine in as many different characters
and costumes as possible; so that we have the advantage of seeing Mdme. Patti as Catarina assume, in the
first place, the dress and demeanour of a Russian
maiden of the humbler class, after which she somehow
becomes transformed into a species of gipsy, and finally
—as regards the first act alone—disappears on her
travels in the disguise of a young man. In the second
act where Peter becomes the prominent and Catarina
almost a subordinate character—at least, until the
dramatic scene in which the young sentinel suddenly
confronts and insults his (or her) much besotted and

entirely mystified chief—the heroine wears uniform and carries a musket. In the third act she is seen in the white muslin dress of young-lady-hood, and the dishevelled hair of gentle lunacy; until, in the final scene of the act, she appears as Empress or Tsarina with the crown of sovereignty on her beautiful head.

If it were not very perfectly played, *L'Etoile du Nord*, with its redundant recitative (substituted for the spoken dialogue of the French original) and its four hours' duration, would, spite of its numerous beauties, be intolerable, considered merely as an entertainment. In other words, it would be anything but entertaining. But Mdme. Patti is so fascinating as the heroine and M. Faure and M. Maurel are both so impressive as the hero that the lengthiness of the second and third acts can be supported for the sake of the scenes in which Catarina or Peter or both of them appear.

In the gipsy rondo, in the duet with Prascovia, in the expressive melody followed by the brilliant barcarolle which brings the first act to a conclusion, in the moving scene within and without the tent in which the unhappy Catarina discovers Peter's infidelity to her and his fidelity to the bottle, Mdme. Patti, from interesting and engaging, becomes intensely dramatic. But her finest performance of all is in the pathetic last act—the most beautiful and by far the most effective of the sufficiently numerous last acts in which melancholy madness is exhibited to us in a graceful shape and is gradually charmed away through the happy associations called up by appropriate music. Apart, moreover, from the admirable manner in which the two principal parts are filled by Mdme. Patti and M. Faure, *L'Etoile du Nord,* as represented at the Royal Italian Opera, is well worth seeing for its spectacular attractions, and well worth hearing for the choral and orchestral ensemble. There is not in any of Meyerbeer's "grand" operas, specially so named, a more remarkable combined effect than is produced in the overpowering finale to the second act by the simultaneous execution of a pretended Russian, but really Prussian march, another march, in different time, by a Cossack fife band (Prussian again in its origin), and a chorus. The celebrated finale in *Don Giovanni* is even more complex; but it is also more harmonious and infinitely less noisy.

The "Opéra Comique" character of the work is quite lost at the Royal Italian Opera, where, for instance, the duet in the form of a duel, or duel in the form of a duet, between the two vivandières, has never been, and is never likely to be, effective. This ingenious little piece is lost in a large theatre, as a Meissonier is lost on the walls of a vast picture gallery. Nor, out of France, is it ever sung with proper spirit. When *L'Etoile du Nord* was first brought out at the Opéra Comique, the duet between the vivandières was the one thing that seemed really to strike what Victor

Hugo once called the "esprit essentiellement vaude-
villiste" of the Parisian public. Many must have heard
this duet better given in France by burlesque actresses,
who had never learned to sing, than by the able vocalists to whom, invariably, it has been entrusted at
the Royal Italian Opera. But nowhere so well as at
the Royal Italian Opera have the grand features of the
work been brought out; and at no other theatre have
the two principal parts been filled by such consummate
artists as Mdme. Adelina Patti and M. Faure.

As a general rule, when a work of the Opéra Comique
type has been adapted to the Italian stage the spoken
dialogue which the traditions, and indeed the strict
regulations, of the Opéra Comique Theatre render indispensable, has been set to long and lumbering recitatives, so that for the sake of lightness one has longed
for the work in its original form, with all its imperfec-
tions in the way of abrupt changes from the speaking
to the singing and from the singing to the speaking
voice. Meyerbeer, in arranging his own *Etoile du Nord*
for the Royal Italian Opera, had a narrow escape of
crushing it beneath the weight of his added recitatives
(which, as the work is now given, are considerably
curtailed); especially in the third act. No wonder,
then, that *Le Domino Noir* and *Les Diamants de la
Couronne* suffered at the hands of the unknown musicians who "with a light heart" undertook the arduous
duty of completing them and to a certain extent trans-

forming them into Italian operas. *Fra Diavolo* is the only one of Auber's works which has had the inestimable advantage of being Italianised by its own composer; and *Fra Diavolo* is apparently the only one of Auber's operas which is destined to maintain its place permanently in the Italian repertory. Herr Wagner has expressed his indignation at the idea of *William Tell* having being made the subject of an Italian opera, when the Germanic character of its incidents—that is to say of its fable—required that it should be treated in German style. Of *Fra Diavolo* it may fairly be said that it is evidently fitted by its subject, characters, and scenery for the Italian stage; and Auber, in the delightful music with which the romantic tale inspired him, has shown himself as much an Italian as a Frenchman.

Dinorah is certainly the most lunatical opera ever composed. From Belisarius and Nebuchadnezzar to the unhistoric Linda and Lucia the lyric drama is full of heroes and heroines who at some period of the opera, and generally in the last act, take leave of their senses; some to become the harmless entertainers of a dear illusion, others to go stark mad. But *Dinora* is the only opera in which all the characters (except the goat) are more or less demented from beginning to end. Corentino is a childish idiot, Hoel a gloomy and superstitious fanatic whose credulity touches closely upon insanity, while the graceful Dinorah is crazy with a craziness which is ideal, no doubt, but is real all the same.

Meyerbeer, it has been said, wrote *Le Pardon de Ploermel* to show that he could dispense with those accessories in the form of processions, ballets, scenery, and stage decorations generally, which, according to some critics, constituted the chief attractions of *Robert le Diable, Les Huguenots,* and *Le Prophète.* He had reckoned, however, without the manager of the Royal Italian Opera, who has given to the charming little idyll many of the features of a fine spectacle. The procession in celebration of the " pardon," without being too grand, is strikingly pretty ; and the scene of the ravine and waterfall, with the fragile bridge above it, forms a most effective stage picture.

Dinorah is a work which, as is generally known, had the comparative and temporary misfortune to be brought out at the Opéra Comique of Paris, for which Meyerbeer specially composed it. Not that it was in-differently performed. On the contrary, the original cast was excellent, including, as it did, Marie Cabel as Dinorah and Faure as Hoel. But the conventions of the theatre, and, indeed, the terms of its license, re-quired that the musical pieces should be separated by a certain amount of spoken dialogue ; and *Le Pardon de Ploermel* or *Dinorah,* as it was afterwards to be called, was not heard in the form which should have belonged to it from the first until Meyerbeer converted it from a hybrid musical drama into an opera properly so called. This desirable change was effected for the Royal Italian Opera, where *Dinorah*, since its first production in Italian, has formed one of the most admired, as it is certainly one of the most admirable, works in the repertory of the theatre. Of late years, too, it has acquired new attractiveness through the part of the heroine being assumed by Mdme. Adelina Patti, whose Dinorah is one of her most poetical impersonations. Those, indeed, who have only seen Mdme. Patti in such very different characters as those of Rosina in *Il Barbiere* and of Leonora in *Il Trovatore* can have no idea of the full range of her histrionic genius unless they have also seen and heard her as Dinorah. There are plenty of fantastic characters in opera ; but of characters at once fantastic, graceful, and consistent, there is scarcely one that can be placed on a level with that of the heroine in *Le Pardon de Ploermel*. She has, thanks to Meyerbeer, her own musical physiognomy, and, thanks to Mdme Patti, her own musical expression. Written for one of the most brilliant vocalists of the period, the part abounds in difficulties which, as treated by Mdme. Patti, are only so many opportunities for the display of consummate facility. Dinorah, as a singer, is passing over the loftiest and slenderest bridges, and by the side of the most dangerous precipices, not in the scene of the cataract alone, but throughout the opera. Apart, too, from dazzling flights in the highest region of the vocal register, she has passages of simple expression, which are not, perhaps, more melodious than those with which they form so striking a contrast, but which are melodious in another manner. What, for instance, can be more beautiful than the lullaby of the first act—as full of tenderness as any of Schubert's songs? "Lullaby to an intractable goat," it might be called; for the ungrateful creature refuses only too often to be caressed by the hand and by the voice of the charmer, even if it does not (as sometimes happens) turn the solo into a duet by introducing from mysterious recesses at the back of the stage unmusical notes of its own. Meyerbeer was fond of animals; and, had he carried out the intention he seems at one time to have entertained of setting "Faust" to music, he would doubtless have added to the horses of *Les Huguenots*, and the goat of *Dinorah*, the dog which so naturally becomes transformed into the cynical Mephistopheles.

Though everything in the opera is finished to the last point, and though Meyerbeer has bestowed as much care on the songs of the episodical characters—the typical personages of country life—and on the choruses which fill up and give colour to the picture as on the leading parts, the dramatic interest is confined to the three agents through whom the story is worked out, and belongs, above all, to Dinorah. It is astonishing, when one reflects on it, in how many and what various moods this interesting heroine is exhibited to us. Tender with the goat, who in the end (thereby asserting his kinship with the goats of Scripture) leads her almost to destruction, playful with Corentin, trustful with Hoel, and thoroughly fascinating in her capricious dealings with the moonlight and with her own shadow, there is something weird-like in her presence and performances throughout. Dinorah suggests, in more than one respect, George Sand's *Petite Fadette.* The part is poetical in itself, and Mdme. Patti invests it, moreover, with a poetry of her own.

CHAPTER XXV.

VERDI, AND FOUR OF HIS OPERAS.

ERNANI, at one time and for many years the most popular of Verdi's works, is scarcely known, except through its leading melodies, to the younger generation of opera-goers. The principal airs from *Ernani* have never ceased to be presented from time to time at concerts; but *Ernani* as a whole seems to have been relegated to the vast limbo of forgotten works. There is nothing old-fashioned in the style of the opera; in parts, indeed, it might have been written in the present day by some violent imitator of Verdi, such as the Brazilian composer Gomez. But it abounds in over-emphatic outbursts, ultra-expressive contrasts, and crudities of various kinds, which force one to conclude that Verdi's early manner was an imperfect manner. He has learned much and forgotten much since the days of *Ernani,* though *Ernani,* all the same, is full of merit, and interesting as one of the most thoroughly characteristic of its composer's works. It abounds in melody of a thoroughly Verdian type; and in much of its vehement music there is the accent of true passion. Such beauty as it undoubtedly possesses met with but little recognition when the work was first presented, under the management of Mr. Lumley, at Her Majesty's Theatre. But though for many years it may have been undervalued it is certainly inferior to the *Ballo in Maschera, Rigoletto,* the *Trovatore,* and in some respects even to the *Traviata.*

There are three of Victor Hugo's plays which, in addition to their dramatic interest, could not fail to engage the attention of composers from certain musical or acoustical effects introduced in the leading situations. Music and musical sounds are employed with terrible suggestiveness in *Lucrezia Borgia, Le Roi s'amuse (Rigoletto),* and *Hernani (Ernani* in the Italian); but the means so effective in the spoken dramas are much less effective, for reasons easy enough to explain, in the operas! In the drama of *Lucrezia Borgia* the speaking voice has alone been heard, until suddenly a funeral dirge is sung outside the windows of Lucrezia's palace. Such a means of arresting attention, exciting emotion, awakening expectation, is infallible—at least in the drama. In the opera, however, where music is not

19 *

brought in by exception but has been the language of the piece throughout, the effect is less striking. In *Le Roi s'amuse* the audience hear one song, sung in the last act, and are naturally much impressed at hearing the same song sung again, in the same voice, by the man whose supposed corpse is actually before them. In an opera, however, it is not at all unusual to hear the principal character sing a song; and in *Rigoletto*, as if to underline the tenor's air, when at the critical moment it is repeated, the composer causes it to be sung without accompaniment. The device, all the same, does not tell in the opera as in the drama. Finally, in *Ernani* the horn, whose significant sounds carry such terror with them in Victor Hugo's play, may in Verdi's opera suggest to the initiated and to students of the libretto what it is intended to suggest. But so many horns, cornets, trombones, and all sorts of brazen instruments, have been blown and blasted in the course of this noisiest of noisy operas, that to make so much fuss about one little horn seems nothing short of ridiculous.

Those who hold that the dramatist is not called upon to invent his own plots, and that he is even required by numerous illustrious examples to abstain from doing so, must entertain but a poor opinion of Victor Hugo, who in *Hernani* produced a drama as remarkable for the interest of its fable as for the beauty of its dialogue. Some of the finest of its many fine dramatic scenes, in losing Victor Hugo's impassioned language, lose everything. But the intrigue is simple, intelligible, and well suited for operatic presentation : and this apart from the horn, which so far as musical effect is concerned, might be replaced by a glove, a dagger, or any other token. The beautiful Elvira, as becomes a lady of such attractive personal appearance, has three lovers, of whom, as becomes a lady of so true a heart, she loves but one. The one she loves is, of course, prevented by insurmountable obstacles from marrying her ; and this at once fortunate and unfortunate man is the proscribed Ernani—conspirator, exile, and bandit. The lover whom circumstances are compelling Elvira to marry is Don Ruy Gomez de Silva, an old gentleman of dignified appearance, who in the well-known air for the baritone, " Infelice," complains with quaint pathos that, having locks of grey, he still feels beneath his breast a youthful heart. Neither Elvira nor, above all, Ernani is inclined to accept this antithesis as a reason for allowing Don Silva to follow the dictates of his juvenile impulse. The King—no less a potentate than Charles V.—is on his side disposed to prevent the marriage ; and when at a particular moment Elvira by an ingenious dramatic combination is thrown into the King's power the two other lovers, the favoured Ernani and the detested Silva, unite to frustrate his Majesty's designs. Meanwhile, however, Ernani has forfeited his life to his hated rival, from whom he accepts the right

of continuing to exist on condition that when the
horn he offers as a pledge to Don Silva is sounded he
will, on hearing its notes, give up his "head"—
which, by the way, in the course of the piece he offers
freely whenever occasion seems to demand or even to
permit the sacrifice.   Towards the end of the work
Charles V. in his grandeur becomes generous.   He
forgives Ernani when the proscribed one has at last
fallen into his hands, and even consents to his union
with that Elvira whom he himself loves.   Ernani and
Elvira are at the summit of happiness, and are engaged
in singing a very beautiful duet when the fatal sound of
Ernani's horn as blown by the revengeful Silva is heard
in the distance.   Silva approaches, and a magnificent
scene occurs, which ends with the death of Ernani,
who kills himself rather than break his word, and
of Elvira, who dies that she may not survive her
over.   Don Silva, with his grey hair and his youthful
heart, is also on the point of dying when the curtain
falls.

Ernani contains no concerted piece comparable for
ingenuity and dramatic effect to the quartet in *Rigoletto*,
or in the quintet in *Un Ballo in Maschera.*   The finale,
however, of the third act, if neither very massive nor
very elaborate, has at least the advantage of being constructed on a thoroughly tuneful theme.   There are
plenty of finales more dramatic, but there is not one
in the whole range of Italian opera more melodious and

more singable than that which brings the third act of Ernani to an end.

It is difficult to understand the passion with which prime donne seem to be inspired for the part of Leonora in *Il Trovatore*. Twenty years ago one might have understood it; but it is scarcely intelligible in the present day when *Il Trovatore* has, more than any other opera, been hacked almost to death. One can only imagine that both Mdme. Patti and Mdme. Nilsson, who have successively adopted the favoured part of Leonora, have done so by way of task, and in order to show that they possess the art of giving freshness to a well-worn character. Mdme. Patti's immense success in this seemingly unpromising enterprise had already been recognised when Mdme. Nilsson proved that she also, instead of confining herself to the more gentle and poetical parts in which she gained her first reputation, could adopt with all due effect the melodramatic gestures and the declamatory style of Verdi's most conventional, and at the same time most inexplicable, heroine. " Had she a father, had she a mother?" &c., one may ask in regard to Leonora as in regard to Violetta herself; the librettist giving no cue whatever either as to her antecedents or her relatives. The Count di Luna had, or fancied he had, certain claims upon her. He may have been her guardian—a sort of romantic Bartolo; in which case Manrico would have to be regarded as a kind of vagrant Almaviva.

But, with the exception of the grotesque gipsy
Azucena—who is very real, very horrible—all the
personages of *Il Trovatore* are "in the air," if not in
the clouds.

The ideal and the conventional give one another too
often the hand; and this is especially the case in *Il
Trovatore* which is at the same time very unreal and
very commonplace. Only two critics—or at most
three—have ever, as far as I know, taken a serious view
of *Il Trovatore*; two (in one) being the authoresses of
an account of travels in Southern Europe profess-
ing to be written by an "unprotected female"; the
third an ingenuous character in one of M. Sardou's
plays. The "unprotected female," finding herself in
Sicily, went into raptures at the idea of being in
the very country where, as she believed, the incidents
of *Il Trovatore* had taken place. The *ingénue* in *Les
Vieux Garçons* has a still firmer faith in the absolute
truth of the story; a fact of which she assures her
amazed parent as, unconscious of his relationship
towards her, he listens attentively and admiringly to her
feeble performance of "Di quella pira" with a wrong
accompaniment. Sardou justly thought that to paint
the extreme of ingenuousness it was only necessary to
represent a young girl as coming away from her first
operatic representation with a lively faith in the genu-
ineness of *Il Trovatore* considered as a drama of real
life. It is not that the events set forth are so

very improbable—those of the *Merchant of Venice,* a *Winter's Tale, Macbeth,* are more improbable by far— but that the characters belong to neither place, time, nor humanity. Spite of this, Verdi has given his operatic puppets life by the vigorous, richly-coloured melodies which he has written for them; and it must be for the sake of the music, not the dramatic interest, of the several parts, that singers of the highest eminence are always found ready to undertake their representation.

The part of Manrico is invariably reserved for tenors of undoubted "robustness"; but that of Leonora has from the first been sung by prime donne of nearly every calibre, from almost the lightest to quite the heaviest.   During the first popularity of the work the most graceful and refined vocalist of her time, the late Mdme. Bosio, played the part very charmingly, without troubling herself much about its dramatic significance or insignificance. But it was Mdme. Grisi who, by force of constant iteration and reiteration, put her stamp upon it so that the public, after a time, came to regard it as the peculiar property of the dramatic, tragic, or, so to say, "robust" soprano. That this was a mistake is sufficiently shown by the fact that the original Leonora of this side of the Alps was Mdme. Frezzolini—a brilliant singer of the light florid school. The Leonora, in fact, of the *Trovatore*—who must not be confounded either with the Leonora of *La Favorita,* nor, above all, with the Leonora of *Fidelio,* both of them parts of real dramatic meaning—is the property of any soprano who likes to take it; though, considering the call it makes, especially in the last act, on the energy and resources of even the most vigorous singers, it is one that by the great majority of prime donne would be best left alone.

It might be objected by historians and ethnologists to the plot of the *Trovatore* that before the gipsies came into Europe troubadours and trouvères had already disappeared. Consequently Manrico and Azucena could not have existed at the same time; whence it follows that the opera of *Il Trovatore* has no basis of existence—in spite of which it lives and thrives, and instead of being less admired is apparently more admired each time it is heard. Few know the meaning of the opera, since to grasp the entire subject it is necessary to arrive early enough for the introductory legend, and to wait until the very end for Azucena's explanatory revelation. It is impossible to define the time, and no one can even imagine the place, in which the action goes on; nor is it clear why Manrico, the troubadour, wears a white stocking on one leg and a red stocking on the other. But everyone can see that there are two men who, as tenor and baritone, and also because they are in love with the same woman, hate each another; and that one of the two has a mother who appears to love her son, until, at the very last moment, it turns out that the sup-

posed son is not her son, and that the supposed mother,
instead of loving her supposed son, detests him, and has
placed him in a position of mortal antagonism towards
his own brother. The story begins with child-murder
and ends with fratricide. But apart from these horrors
the piece presents many striking situations, many
picturesque contrasts; and it thus possesses a certain
dramatic merit apart from the large number of agreeable and often beautiful melodies which Verdi has introduced into it. The tunes, however, made the success
of the *Trovatore* in England; and it has now attained
that firm position of favour which awaits every
thoroughly tuneful opera when its music has been performed for some twenty-five years entire and in fragments, in all sorts of shapes and on all sorts of instruments and combinations of instruments, from the
operatic orchestra to the street-beggar's clarinet.

If it were as easy as some suppose to give to a dramatic personage a special musical physiognomy, how
tired the frequenters of the opera would by this
time have become of gipsy operas! In *Maritana* the
heroine is a gipsy; in the *Bohemian Girl*, the heroine
is, of course, a gipsy—not a " Bohemian " at all, but
" une Bohémienne "; in the *Trovatore* both the hero
and the female villain of the piece are gipsies. Verdi's
Azucena is incomparably more dramatic, has infinitely
more character, than Wallace's Maritana and Balfe's
Arline. But that the sort of character which marks

Verdi's malicious and vengeful hag is gipsy character
it would be very unsafe to affirm; while it can be stated
without the least fear of contradiction that neither the
gipsy of Wallace nor the gipsy of Balfe possesses one
recognisable gipsy characteristic. Fancy a gipsy singing "Scenes that are brightest" or " I dreamt that I
dwelt in marble halls ! " In setting *Preciosa* to music
—of which the story is virtually the same as that of
the *Bohemian Girl,* both being derived from Cer-
vantes' *Gipsy of Madrid*—Weber, with his dramatic
genius, could not help endeavouring in some measure
to gipsify the subject. But one great difficulty which
must always stand in the way of attempting to introduce
gipsy music into gipsy operas arises from the fact that
no such thing as gipsy music exists. The so-called
gipsy march in *Preciosa* is quite gipsy enough for
dramatic purposes; but it is in fact Arab.

The gipsies have strong musical and dramatic in-
stincts; but all endeavours to show that they possess a
music of their own—a music of gipsy origin and peculiar
to gipsies—have hitherto failed. In Russia gipsies
sing, in Hungary they play the violin, in Spain they
sing and dance; but they adopt in each case for their
performances the airs of the country they are living in.
Liszt, in his partly anecdotal, partly fantastic, for the
most part rhapsodical, work on " The Gipsies and their
Music in Hungary," says boldly that the gipsies have
a music of their own based on a different scale from

ours. But Hungarian critics, in noticing the work when it first appeared, pointed out that the melodies played by Hungarian gipsies, which struck Liszt as so peculiarly gipsy, were in fact Hungarian; while as regards scale, the Hungarians use the ordinary one, only departing from it now and then, when, in spite of themselves, they play wrong notes. There is no such thing as gipsy music, just as there is no such thing as Jewish music; though both Jews and gipsies are specially distinguished by musical abilities—the latter more generally; the former in fewer cases, but more highly.

With the exception of the Jewish pedlar in *La Gazza Ladra* and the distinguished Hebrews who figure in *Mosè in Egitto*, no Jews are to be found in opera; whereas in half the lyric dramas of the period one or more gipsies are presented. Besides the *Bohemian Girl, Maritana,* and the *Trovatore,* there are gipsies in Verdi's *Traviata, La Forza del Destino, Rigoletto,* and *Ballo in Maschera,* as well as in Meyerbeer's *Etoile du Nord* and *Huguenots.* Auber, too, was fond of gipsies; and it is quite possible that Scribe, the favourite librettist of Auber and of Meyerbeer, may be chiefly responsible for their introduction on the lyric stage. Rossini, Donizetti, and Bellini knew nothing of gipsies. Nor does a gipsy turn up in any one of Mozart's operas; not even in the *Magic Flute,* which comprises so many strange characters of the most varied kinds. The music sung by the operatic gipsy—when the composer aims seriously at character and colour—is usually of a Spanish cast. But the gipsies of English operas—our Maritanas and our Bohemian Girls—sing ballads of the usual Bond-street pattern, resembling in that all the other characters in works of the same class.

Il Trovatore was played for the first time on this side of the Alps at the Italian Theatre of Paris in 1854 or 1855, with Signor Baucardé as Manrico, Mdme. Borghi-Mamo as Azucena, and Mdme. Frezzolini as Leonora. Since those days *Il Trovatore* has been heard a good many times in Paris, in London, and in St. Petersburg—the three great capitals of Italian opera—with excellent casts. Wherever it has been best played the favourite Count di Luna has always been Signor Graziani; and not one season has passed at the Royal Italian Opera since 1855 without Signor Graziani appearing as that jealous Provençal Count with whom he has so completely identified himself. The choruses in *Il Trovatore* are not particularly admirable in a scientific point of view; but they are rhythmical, melodious, and exceedingly effective.

The reason why everyone made an outcry when *La Traviata* was produced, while no one ever found fault with the morality of *La Favorita,* is to be found, no doubt, in the fact, not that the heroine is very much better in the latter work than in the former, but that in the one the manners are openly dissolute throughout, while in the other they are at least based on the ordinary notions of decorum. King Alphonso, himself the worst character in the piece, is more feeble than wicked; and, the occasion presenting itself, does not omit to pay to virtue the homage due to it from vice. In *La Traviata*, on the other hand, we see vice in the character of Violetta receiving homage from virtue as personified in the elder Germont; and although Violetta suffers a good deal in the course of the drama, she is never rebuked for her general mode of life, but only for her unfaithful conduct towards one particular admirer who is moved to upbraid her, not by love of virtue, but merely by wounded self-love.

It is useless, however, to write homilies on the subject of frailty as exhibited in the character of Violetta. That form of weakness, relieved here and there by bursts of hysterical strength, is not disliked by operatic audiences; while prime donne, especially soprani of the appropriately "light" type, absolutely delight in it. Violetta is a part which is gradually becoming historical, and which has long possessed recognised traditions. It, indeed, possesses two sets of traditions; according to one of which Violetta is very demonstrative, coughs as she sings, and dies coughing; while, according to the other, she is very quiet and refined, and expires without making one distinctive phthisical sign.

A key to the view taken of the character of Violetta by the artist representing it is always afforded by the champagne song of the first scene. Mdme. Nilsson, in singing this air, is but moderately reckless, and abstains from spilling any of her wine. Mdme. Patti spills a few drops, which the audience are apparently intended to regard as the result of an accident, since an obliging gentleman at once comes forward and fills the partially depleted glass. Others throw the whole contents of the glass to the ground—which one may venture to say is not even realistic; since Violetta, in a state of genuine bacchanalian ecstasy, though she might fling her glass to the ground, would not do so until she had swallowed its contents. The realistic interpretation of such a character ought not to be attempted at all. At least, the artist who takes this part—which makes more demand on the taste than on the talent of its representative— should remember that Violetta is not a typical but altogether an exceptional personage. Otherwise no one would ever have dreamt of writing, or of dramatising, or of setting music to her melancholy history, which is known to have been in its main incidents a true one. Particulars on this subject may be found not only in M. Alexandre Dumas's preface to *La Dame aux Camélias*, but also in Mr. Forster's *Life of Dickens*; for Dickens, long before the publication of *La Dame aux Camélias*, had conceived the idea of treating in the form of a novel the history of the ill-fated girl who became, in the hands of Alexandre Dumas *fils*, Margaret Gautier, and in those of Verdi and his librettist Violetta Valery. There are certain details in the novel of *La Dame aux Camélias* which would be intolerable in the drama, and certain details in the drama which, whether intolerable or not, are very properly omitted in the opera.

This, by the way, explains what the dramatic licenser is said to have found very difficult to account for in his examination some years ago before the Committee of the House of Commons : the fact that the Italian operatic version of *La Dame aux Camélias* is allowed to be represented, while the sanction of the Lord Chamberlain has been refused to English prose translations of the same drama. The official theory on the subject is that what might be very dangerous in English, is harmless enough in Italian, for the simple reason that Italian, even to most opera-goers, is an unknown tongue. It is a positive fact that at Exeter Hall the directors did on one occasion object to the airs from *La Traviata* being sung in English, and afterwards allowed them to be sung in Italian.

One must admit, however, that there is an immense difference, morally speaking, between the opera of *La Traviata* and the drama of *La Dame aux Camélias*. The former contains all the sentiment to be found in the latter, but none of the manners; and *La Dame aux Camélias* is really so full of the manners of vicious life that it deserves to be looked upon as a wicked sort of comedy rather than as a drama. The inferior *"traviata,"* who in the drama borrows a hundred francs from her richer but more consumptive friend, promising to pay her in two days, when she knows she cannot live twelve hours, becomes, in the opera, the absolutely colourless Flora Bervoix, who borrows nothing from anyone, and for whom Signor Verdi has not even taken the trouble to borrow a phrase of melody. Take away the not very dreadful gambling scene and the by no means alarming ball scene, and Alfredo and Violetta might almost be Paul and Virginia living in the City of Paris instead of the Isle of France. Numbers of English young ladies who go to hear *La Traviata* and who even sing " Ah fors' e lui," themselves, in their own delightful manner, are convinced that Violetta's fault consists only in this ; that she goes out too much to balls, behaves flightily when she is at them, and has no dowry. For these reasons, or rather for the last reason, old Germont will not allow his son to marry her ; and the grief and despair which ensue are looked upon as the natural and inevitable consequences of a sudden interruption of the course of true love. The music does, perhaps, here and there throw a veil over a situation of which the true nature would be indicated by the words if they could only be heard ; but speaking generally, it is because the drama has been turned into an opera, not because the French has been turned into Italian, that *La Traviata* is inoffensive as compared with *La Dame aux Camélias.* There exists a purified

American version of *La Dame aux Camélias* called *Camille the Coquette*; and it is no more a libel on the Lady with the Camelias to call her a " coquette" than it would be to speak of Messalina as " a terrible flirt." But probably the story, even as it has been pared down by the librettist to meet the requirements of the composer, would still not be tolerable to a decent English audience had not the outline been softened and the whole expression transfigured through music.

A prima donna of taste does not attempt to depict the physical side of the illness to which Violetta is destined to succumb. She endeavours to represent her moral sufferings alone. Here, again, one cannot help comparing the opera with the drama and with the novel. The symptoms of consumption, which are unflinchingly delineated in the novel, are somewhat softened down in the play. In the opera the physical details altogether disappear.

Operatic fashions are as much beyond the control of criticism as the fashions of every-day life; and the prima donna, like every other lady, will continue, whatever may be written on the subject, to attire herself as she may think, and as a rule in obedience to the dictates of her own particular taste. Violetta in *La Traviata* dresses in the very latest style; so that from year to year we see her appear in costumes of new make, and always in accordance with the most recent fashions. Alfredo, however, and the venerable Germont wear the costume of the eighteenth century;

and they might, without incurring much blame, wear that of the seventeenth or any earlier age.

"What a part you are going to play to-night!" said some one to an actress who was about to appear as Lady Macbeth.

"Yes, it is a good part," replied the lady, "I wear four different dresses in it."

That is precisely the case with Violetta. Two ball-dresses, a morning-dress, and a night-gown (for which a peignoir may be substituted) are indispensable for the correct impersonation of *La Traviata*; and the ball-dresses should both be as magnificent as art and money can make them. The opportunity given by the part for a display of elaborate toilettes has something, no doubt, to do with the favour in which it is held by prime donne, who are women first and singers afterwards, and who, being women, cannot be insensible to the attractions of dress. The character, moreover, in a dramatic point of view, presents the greatest advantages. All the interest is centred in the heroine. No one cares an atom what happens to anyone else. Old Germont may disinherit young Germont, young Germont may break old Germont's heart—though that would probably be difficult; the fate of Violetta is the one thing that claims our attention, and everything else in the drama is indifferent to us. To take a stage-manager's view of the matter, Violetta is "on" in every scene. She begins and ends the first act, ends the second act, and has the whole of the third act to herself. All the other parts together have not so much music in them as is contained in that of Violetta; which, moreover, compared, not with other parts in the same opera, but with other prima donna parts, even those of the first magnitude, is unusually full of solos in various shapes.

It is not astonishing, then, that *débutantes* should like to appear as Violetta, though matter for surprise may still be found in the constant succession of Violettas presented to us. Alfredo is a weak-minded and in many respects contemptible lover; while as for Germont the elder, the character, in a moral sense, suffers sadly from the necessity felt by the librettist and composer of exhibiting him for the sake of the concerted music in scenes where, except for purely lyrical reasons, it would be better he should not appear.

The opera of *La Traviata* has hitherto enjoyed in England a career more or less in correspondence with that of Violetta herself up to the moment of Violetta's greatest happiness; when she first becomes aware of Alfredo's devotion to her. In the beginning the British public had as bad an opinion of *La Traviata* as Alfredo at the outset had, it may be presumed, of Violetta. But though fundamentally worthless, *La Traviata* presents some good and many brilliant points; and the opera has gradually gained our toleration, our sympathy, and finally our liking. Thus Alfredo, in the presence of Violetta, learned first to endure, then pity, then embrace. Whether *La Traviata* will some day fall in public estimation, and ultimately perish from this species of decline, remains to be seen. But it has at present only reached the brindisi-singing, champagne-drinking stage of its existence. The morality of M. Dumas the younger's most popular work has been more than sufficiently discussed; with the usual result, after a prolonged debate, of leaving the question a little more obscure than when it was first brought forward. The opera is comparatively harmless. But the drama, or serious comedy, on which it is founded, is, in a great measure, what the opera is not, a study of manners, and of manners which certainly cannot be studied with advantage. Besides throwing a halo of sentiment round the heroine, who is sure to be regarded by a large portion of the audience not as a rare exception, but as a type of the class to which she belongs, the drama keeps the spectators for several hours in the worst possible society; with the natural effect produced, according to Menander and to St. Paul, by "evil communications" on "good manners." In the opera the objectionable sentiment is, of course, preserved; but the odious realism of the play is lost, to the great benefit of the work in a moral point of view. Violetta in *La Traviata* is no more offensive than *Cleopatra*—that "*reine entretenue*," as Heine calls her—in Shakspere's tragedy.

Un Ballo in Maschera is one of Verdi's finest operas. Years ago most English amateurs would have ranked it next to *Rigoletto*, and it is Verdi's own fault if, now that *Aïda*—certainly Verdi's masterpiece—has been heard, *Uu Ballo in Maschera* could only be classed, in the spirited competition which the composer has carried on with himself through his own works, as " a good third." Few operas demand such a strong cast as *Un Ballo in Maschera*. It contains no fewer than five leading parts. But it is nearly impossible to present in one and the same piece five characters all equally interesting ; and of the vocal personages who make up the quintet of *Un Ballo* two—the mezzo soprano and the contralto—attract less attention and excite less sympathy than the light soprano, the tenor, and the baritone. The light-soprano part, to begin at the top, is the most brilliant that Verdi has written. His genius is mainly of a sombre and melodramatic character. In the part of Oscar, however, he has struck a new vein. Here he is not only brilliant—which in a serious way he has shown himself in many of his operas —but lively, gay, and full of an abandonment one might well have thought foreign to his somewhat gloomy nature. It must have been by an effort and by a determination not to let himself be outshone by the French composer who had treated the same subject and the same characters before him, that Verdi succeeded in making his page as vivacious as the page Auber had presented in *Gustave III.* and more melodious. No professed cultivator of the lighter style of opera has written a more graceful or more tuneful air

than the one to which Oscar sings his (or her) couplets in the final scene of *Un Ballo in Maschera.*

Amalia is not a part for which prime donne are in
the habit of contending. No prima donna ever had a
clause inserted in her engagement to the effect that
she alone should appear as Amalia in *Un Ballo in
Maschera.* Amalia, however, has plenty of good stirring
dramatic work assigned to her, and she has much agitated music to sing. The duet for Amalia and the
Duke is dramatic enough ; and in various scenes Amalia
has a fair proportion of effective phrases to deliver.
But the composer has given her no such scena as he
has bestowed upon the heroines of *Ernani, Il Trovatore,* and so many other of his operas. The French
literary gourmand compared a dessert without cheese
to a woman with only one eye. The idea of a fatal
want might have been more gracefully conveyed by the
example of a prima donna's part in an Italian opera
without a cavatina.

The contralto part must, like the part of the prima
donna, be classed with those known as "ungrateful."
It requires much; it gives but little in return. The
sorceress Ulrica is very inferior to the gipsy Azucena.
She is scarcely superior, as regards interest, to that
other gipsy, Maddalena, in *Rigoletto.*

Oscar is but an incidental character, though in the
last act the vivacious and brightly-singing page acquires
a certain dramatic importance when, bearing the invitation to the fatal ball, he suddenly appears as the

messenger of destiny. But in a musical point of view the part of Oscar is, as before observed, a leading one throughout the opera. It is made up, indeed, of a series of sparkling and melodious airs. The high soprano voice of the page counts, moreover, for much in the admirable quintet of the fortune-telling scene.

Many plays have been written for the sake of a single situation ; and the one situation to which *Gustave III.* and *Un Ballo in Maschera* owe their existence is that of the masquerade, where, in the midst of brilliant and almost riotous festivities, the ruling prince is assassinated. Such an incident could not fail to strike the imagination of a dramatist ; and Scribe saw that to produce the fullest possible effect the culminating scene must be presented in operatic form. A ball without music would be impossible. A ball with the dance tunes interrupted from time to time by spoken dialogue would have been sufficiently like reality ; but the operatic mode of treatment, with no very appreciable sacrifice of reality, would give far better artistic results. When the agitated recitative of the conspirators and the subdued strains of the graceful but frivolous dance tune are heard together, the dramatic significance of the scene is brought out very forcibly by the simplest musical means—a proof that the situation is essentially a musical one. In the ball-room, as in one of Heine's songs, " sun and moon and stars are laughing." But there is something beneath the laughter. " Und ich

I.   21

lache auch—und sterbe," the victim might add. The music, in fact, says that for him.

The ball scene in *Un Ballo in Maschera* cannot, of course, be regarded as one of Verdi's greatest achievements in the way of dramatic music. The scene is dramatic in itself, and all the composer had to do was not to spoil it; which he certainly has not done. It is pleasant, however, to find our usually somewhat gloomy composer brightening with the occasion, and writing the liveliest and prettiest dance tunes and the most captivating little ballads, such as the one he has given in this scene to Miss Oscar, the girlish page with the light and agile soprano voice. The Duke, by the way, dies, or at least is stabbed, to the music of a polka-mazurka. Here Strauss or Gung'l might detect an anachronism; which Verdi seems equally to have committed in the ball scene of the first act of *La Traviata*, where Violetta Valery's friends do nothing but waltz; and again in the first act of *Rigoletto* where a minuet is introduced. Minuets were not danced in the days of Francis I., otherwise the Duke of Mantua; nor waltzes in the gilded saloons of Paris during the eighteenth century, to which Violetta, notwithstanding her dresses of last week's fashion and her taste for champagne, is supposed to belong; nor polka-mazurkas anywhere until within the last twenty-five years. It would be well, however, if operas were never inconsistent except in regard to the ballet music. It would be well also if in *Un Ballo in Maschera* that work were

left as the composer wrote it, without the interpolation
in the ball scene of a certain amount of conventional
dance music, which Verdi, of course, did not write and
for which it is not fair to make him responsible. Besides being out of keeping with the rest of the music,
the introduced ballet scene delays the action.

What, it may be asked, was the true name of the
" Duke " in Verdi's unlocalized opera ?   If the Italian
librettist was condemned by a censorship, now happily
abolished, to change his Italian grand duke into an
English governor of Boston, Verdi was not called upon
to Americanise his music; and the melodies of *Un
Ballo in Maschera* are often as unmistakably Italian as
are the costumes of the piece.   But for this excellent
peculiarity it might be suggested that the action of the
piece should take place at Stockholm, where the incidents occurred on which it is known to be founded.   The
French opera-book on which Verdi's opera is based, was
(rare fault for a libretto!) only too truthful.   Otherwise, indeed, the *Gustave III.* of Auber might to this
moment have held the stage.   The sight, however, of a
king murdered in his palace by one of his own
subjects, even as a real king not many years before
had notoriously been slain, was considered a most un-
edifying spectacle for a Parisian public ; and accordingly
a work which many declare to be its composer's masterpiece was abruptly removed from the boards—or rather
was reduced at one " cut " to the final scene of the
masked ball, with the part of Gustavus, and conse-

quently the murder of Gustavus, omitted. When *Gustave III.* was first produced, the wife of Anker-ström is said to have been among the audience, and, according to a story which may or may not be true, a gentleman who had taken an active part in the con-spiracy against the life of his Sovereign wrote to the stage-manager of the opera, to point out that the repre-sentation of the tragic incident in the piece was in certain respects inexact. Count Ankerström, said this realistic critic (who at least spoke with authority on his own particular point), had wounded Gustavus, not in the right side, but in the left. He might, too, have pointed out that the Countess Ankerström did not play in connection with the affair the part attributed to the prima donna, Amalia—that mysterious lady without a surname, wife of Renato, who, on his side, is Renato, and nothing else. Fifty years have elapsed since Auber's *Gustave III.* was originally brought out; and there can be now no reason why it should not be per-formed precisely as Scribe designed the work.

END OF VOL. I.

London: Printed by W. H. Allen & Co., 13 Waterloo Place, Pall Mall.

www.ingramcontent.com/pod-product-compliance
Lightning Source LLC
Chambersburg PA
CBHW021215270326
41929CB00010B/1146